Salads

BLOOMSBURY KITCHEN LIBRARY

Salads

Bloomsbury Books
London

This edition published 1994 by Bloomsbury Books,
an imprint of The Godfrey Cave Group,
42 Bloomsbury Street, London, WC1B 3QJ.

ISBN 1 85471 502 X

Printed and bound in Great Britain.

Contents

Potato Salad with Peas and Sesame Seeds

Serves 8 as a side dish		Calories 140
Working time: about 25 minutes		Protein 3g
		Cholesterol 0mg
Total time: about 1 hour and 15 minutes		Total fat 6g
		Saturated fat 1g
		Sodium 70mg

750 g	waxy potatoes	**1¼ lb**
500 g	fresh peas, shelled, or 150 g (5 oz) frozen peas, thawed	**1 lb**
3 tbsp	sesame seeds	**3 tbsp**
½ tsp	cumin seeds	**½ tsp**
¼ tsp	cayenne pepper	**¼ tsp**
250 g	cucumber, peeled and chopped	**8 oz**

5	spring onions, thinly sliced	**5**
3 tbsp	fresh lemon juice	**3 tbsp**
¼ tsp	salt	**¼ tsp**
2 tbsp	safflower oil	**2 tbsp**
¼ tsp	turmeric	**¼ tsp**
2	mildly hot green chili peppers, seeded deribbed and quartered lengthwise	**2**

Boil the potatoes until they are soft – about 25 minutes. Remove the potatoes from the water, halve them and set them aside to cool.

Parboil the fresh peas until they are tender – 4 to 5 minutes – or briefly blanch the frozen peas. Drain the peas and set them aside.

Heat a small, heavy frying pan over medium-high heat. When hot, add the sesame seeds, half of the cumin seeds and the cayenne pepper; toast the seeds, stirring, until the sesame seeds turn light gold – about 1 minute. Transfer the mixture to a large bowl and let the seeds cool.

Peel the potatoes, then cut them into slices about 8 mm (⅓ inch) thick; halve the slices, and put them in the bowl with the sesame seed

mixture. Grind the remaining cumin with a mortar and pestle and sprinkle it over the potatoes. Add the peas, cucumber, spring onions, lemon juice and salt to the bowl. Toss the ingredients well to combine them, and set aside.

Heat the safflower oil in a heavy frying pan over medium-high heat. When the oil is hot, reduce the heat to low and stir in the turmeric; add the chili peppers and sauté them, stirring, for 1 minute. Remove the chili peppers and reserve them, and pour the contents of the pan over the potato mixture. Stir the salad gently, then transfer it to a serving platter. Garnish the salad with the reserved chilies. The salad may be served at room temperature or chilled.

Greens with Violets and Wild Strawberries

Serves 4 as a first course or a side dish		
Working time: about 10 minutes		
Total time: about 15 minutes		

Calories 60		
Protein 1g		
Cholesterol 0mg		
Total fat 5g		
Saturated fat 1g		
Sodium 25mg		

1 tbsp	raspberry vinegar	1 tbsp	250 g	mixed salad greens, washed and dried	8 oz
1 tbsp	finely chopped shallot	1 tbsp	4 tbsp	sweet violet blossoms (optional)	4 tbsp
½ tsp	Dijon mustard	½ tsp	4 tbsp	wild strawberries (optional)	4 tbsp
	freshly ground black pepper				
1½ tbsp	unsalted chicken stock	1½ tbsp			
1½ tbsp	virgin olive oil	1½ tbsp			

Combine the vinegar, shallot, mustard and some pepper in a small bowl. Let the mixture stand for 5 minutes; whisk in the stock, then the oil. Toss the greens with the dressing. Strew the violets and the strawberries, if using, over the top; serve immediately.

Editor's Note: The greens here include Batavian endive, chicory, watercress and red oakleaf lettuce; any similar combination of mild and bitter greens would be appropriate.

Violet blossoms, when available, add a delicious delicacy to a simple green salad. Pick the blossoms just before serving time. Do not use violets from a florist – they may have been sprayed with chemicals.

Red Cabbage Salad with Spiced Vinegar Dressing

Serves 6
as a
side dish

Working
time: about
15 minutes

Total time:
about
1 hour and
15 minutes

Calories
100
Protein
3g
Cholesterol
0mg
Total fat
8g
Saturated fat
2g
Sodium
170mg

350 g	red cabbage, finely shredded	12 oz
½ tsp	salt	½ tsp
4 tbsp	red wine vinegar	4 tbsp
1	blade of mace	1
1	bay leaf	1
8	peppercorns	8
½ tsp	mustard seeds	½ tsp
4	allspice	4
1	small sweet green pepper, seeded, deribbed and finely sliced	1
2	dried red chili peppers	2
1	small onion, halved and finely sliced	1
3	sticks celery, finely sliced	3
30 g	pine-nuts, lightly toasted	1 oz
2 tbsp	virgin olive oil	2 tbsp
1	garlic clove, crushed	1
¼ tsp	sugar	¼ tsp
	freshly ground black pepper	

Put the shredded cabbage into a large salad bowl, sprinkle with the salt and toss lightly together. Cover the bowl and set it aside in a cool place for 1 hour.

Meanwhile, put the vinegar into a small saucepan with the mace, bay leaf, peppercorns, allspice and chili peppers. Bring to the boil, then boil gently until the vinegar is reduced to 1 tablespoonful. Allow to cool. Add the sliced green pepper, onion, celery and toasted pine-nuts to the red cabbage.

Strain the cold vinegar into a small bowl and add the oil, garlic, sugar and freshly ground pepper to taste. Whisk lightly together. Pour this dressing over the red cabbage and toss well. Serve at once.

Wrapped Salads

Serves 6
as a
first course

Working
time: about
1 hour

Total time:
about
1 hour and
45 minutes

Calories
85

Protein
2g

Cholesterol
0mg

Total fat
4g

Saturated fat
0g

Sodium
220mg

2	fennel bulbs, green tops removed, bulbs cut into bâtonnets	2
250 g	turnips, peeled and cut into bâtonnets	8 oz
500 g	courgettes, cut into bâtonnets	1 lb
2	oranges, juice of 1, pared rind of both	2
6	large Savoy cabbage leaves	6
1	small red onion, finely chopped	1
1½ tbsp	safflower oil	1½ tbsp
2 tbsp	finely chopped fresh chervil or parsley	2 tbsp
½ tsp	salt	½ tsp
	freshly ground black pepper	
6	sprigs fresh chervil or parsley for garnish	6

Bring 2 litres (3½ pints) of water to the boil. Place the fennel in a sieve; lower the sieve part way into the boiling water and blanch until they are tender but still slightly crunchy – 2 to 3 mins. Refresh the fennel under cold water, drain, and transfer it to a large bowl. Blanch the turnip the same way for 2 to 3 mins; refresh, and transfer them to the bowl. Blanch the courgettes for about 1 min; refresh, and put them in the bowl.

Blanch the orange rind in the boiling water for 10 seconds; refresh under cold water and drain. Finely chop and transfer it to the bowl.

Boil the cabbage in the same water until pliable – about 15 seconds. Drain, cool. Remove the thick core from the stem end of each leaf. Set the leaves aside.

Add the onion, oil, orange juice, chopped chervil or parsley, salt and some pepper to the bowl with the bâtonnets; toss the mixture well, then refrigerate for about 15 mins.

Spread the cabbage leaves out on a work surface. Using a slotted spoon, divide the salad evenly among the leaves. Gather the edges of a leaf over its filling; gently twist the edges closed, forming a pouch.Repeat the process.

Place the bundles in a shallow dish and pour the remaining dressing over the top of each. Chill for about 30 mins, garnish with thechervil.

Carrot, Swede and Watercress Salad

Serves 6 as a side dish

Working (and total) time: about 40 minutes

Calories 60
Protein 1g
Cholesterol 0mg
Total fat 3g
Saturated fat 0g
Sodium 70mg

4 tsp	virgin olive oil	**4 tsp**
3	carrots, halved lenthwise, the halves cut diagonally into 5 mm (¼ inch) slices	**3**
325 g	swedes, peeled and cut into bâtonnets	**11 oz**
1	shallot, halved, the halves quartered	**1**

¼ tsp	salt	**¼ tsp**
¼ tsp	cayenne pepper	**¼ tsp**
	freshly ground black pepper	
4 tbsp	cider vinegar	**4 tbsp**
1	bunch of watercress, stemmed, washed and dried	**1**

Heat the oil in a large, heavy frying pan over medium heat. When the oil is hot, add the carrots, swedes, shallot, salt, cayenne pepper and some black pepper. Cook the mixture, stirring frequently, until the vegetables are tender but still crisp – about 7 minutes. Pour the vinegar into the pan and continue cooking, stirring frequently, until almost all of the vinegar has evaporated – 1 to 2 minutes. Stir in the watercress and cook it until it has just wilted – about 30 seconds. Transfer the salad to a serving plate and let it cool just slightly before serving it.

Cucumber and Citrus Salad

Serves 4
as a
side dish

Working
(and total)
time: about
25 minutes

Calories
80

Protein
2g

Cholesterol
0mg

Total fat
1g

Saturated fat
0g

Sodium
135mg

1	large cucumber, cut into 5 cm (2 inch) long segments	1
1 tsp	virgin olive oil	1 tsp
1 tsp	chopped fresh rosemary, or $\frac{1}{4}$ tsp crushed dried rosemary freshly ground black pepper	1 tsp
1	pink grapefruit	1
2	large juicy oranges	2

2 tbsp	fresh lime juice	2 tbsp
4 tbsp	fresh orange juice	4 tbsp
4 tbsp	fresh grapefruit juice	4 tbsp
1 tsp	red wine vinegar	1 tsp
$\frac{1}{4}$ tsp	salt	$\frac{1}{4}$ tsp
1	spring onion, cut into 5 cm (2 inch) long julienne	1

Using an apple corer, a mellon baller or a small spoon remove the core of seeds from each cucumber segment. Slice the segments into rings about 3 mm ($\frac{1}{8}$ inch) thick. Toss the rings with the oil, rosemary and a generous grinding of pepper.

Working over a bowl to catch the juice, cut away the peel, white pith and outer membrane from the grapefruit and oranges. To seperate the segments from the inner membranes, slice down to the core with a sharp knife on either side of each segment; set the segments aside. Cut each

grapefruit segment in half; leave the orange segments whole. Set the bowl containing the juice aside.

Arrange the cucumber slices in a large, deep plate and position the citrus segments on top. If you are preparing the salad in advance, it may be refrigerated for up to 2 hours at this point.

Combine the lime juice, orange juice, grapefruit juice, vinegar and salt with the reserved juice in the bowl. Pour this dressing over the salad; scatter the spring onion over the top just before serving.

Asparagus and Jerusalem Artichoke Salad

Serves 4
as a first
course

Working
(and total)
time: about
20 minutes

Calories
45
Protein
2g
Cholesterol
0mg
Total fat
1g
Saturated fat
0g
Sodium
5mg

1	lemon, cut in half	**1**
125 g	Jerusalem artichokes, scrubbed well	**4 oz**
500 g	asparagus, trimmed, peeled and cut diagonally into 4 cm (1½ inch) lengths	**1 lb**

1 tsp	walnut oil or virgin olive oil	**1 tsp**
1 tbsp	cut fresh dill	**1 tbsp**

Make acidulated water by squeezing the juice of a lemon half into a small bowl of cold water. Peel and slice the Jerusalem artichokes, dropping them into the water as you work.

Pour enough water into a saucepan to fill it about 2.5 cm (1 inch) deep. Set a vegetable steamer in the pan and bring the water to the boil. Put the artichoke slices into the steamer, cover the pan tightly, and steam the slices until they are tender when pierced with a knife – about 5 minutes. Transfer the slices to a bowl and toss them with the juice of the other lemon half.

While the artichokes are steaming, cook the asparagus. Pour enough water into a large, sauté pan to fill it about 2.5 cm (1 inch) deep. Bring the water to the boil, add the asparagus pieces, and cook them until they are tender – about 4 minutes. Drain the asparagus and refresh the pieces under cold water. Drain the pieces once again and toss them with the oil.

Arrange the asparagus on a large serving platter or on four small plates. Top the asparagus with the artichoke slices; sprinkle the dill over all before serving.

Julienned Carrots, Mange-Tout and Chicory

Serves 6
as a first
course or
side dish

Working
(and total)
time: about
20 minutes

Calories
60
Protein
2g
Cholesterol
0mg
Total fat
4g
Saturated fat
0g
Sodium
70mg

1 tbsp	very finely chopped shallot	1 tbsp
1	garlic clove, lightly crushed	1
1 tbsp	herb vinegar or white wine vinegar	1 tbsp
1½ tbsp	almond oil or walnut oil	1½ tbsp

⅛ tsp	salt	⅛ tsp
	freshly ground black pepper	
75 g	carrots, julienned	2½ oz
150 g	mange-tout, julienned	5 oz
250 g	chicory, cored and julienned	8 oz

In a large bowl, combine the shallot, garlic and vinegar. Whisk in the oil and season the dressing with the salt and some pepper. Set the dressing aside while you prepare the vegetables.

Add the carrot julienne to 1 litre (1¾ pints) of boiling water and cook it for 1 minute. Add the mange-tout and cook the vegetables for only 15 seconds longer. Briefly refresh the vegetables under cold running water, then drain them well. Remove the garlic from the dressing and discard it. Add the cooked vegetables and the chicory to the dressing. Toss the salad well and serve it immediately.

Six-Treasure Asian Medley

350 g	carrots	12 oz
125 g	mange-tout, strings removed	4 oz
350 g	small cucumbers	12 oz
4 tbsp	sliced water chestnuts	4 tbsp
250 g	Chinese cabbage, sliced crosswise into 1 cm (½ inch) thick strips	8 oz
1	sweet red pepper, seeded, deribbed and julienned	1

Ginger-Sesame Dressing		
1 tsp	Sichuan peppercorns	1 tsp
1 tsp	dry mustard	1 tsp
2 tsp	sugar	2 tsp
3 tbsp	rice vinegar	3 tbsp
3 tbsp	low-sodium soy sauce or shoyu	3 tbsp
2 tsp	dark sesame oil	2 tsp
2 tbsp	safflower oil	2 tbsp
1 tbsp	finely chopped fresh ginger root	1 tbsp
3	garlic cloves, finely chopped	3

With a small knife, cut a shallow groove running the length of each carrot. Repeat on the opposite side, then slice diagonally into ovals about 3mm (⅛ inch) thick. Put the pieces in a saucepan and pour in enough cold water to cover them by about 5 cm (2 inches). Bring to the boil. Reduce and simmer until barely tender – about 2 mins. Drain and transfer to a bowl.

Cut a V-shaped notch in each end of each mange-tout. Blanch in boiling water for 30 secs. Refresh, drain, add to the bowl with the carrots.

Peel the cucumbers, leaving four narrow strips of skin attached to each one. Halve them lengthwise; scoop out the seeds. Cut the halves into 3 mm (⅛ inch) thick slices. Add the cucumber slices, chestnuts, cabbage and red pepper to the carrots and mange-tout.

To prepare the dressing, put the peppercorns into a small frying pan over medium-high heat. Cook until you see the first wisps of smoke. Transfer to a mortar and crush with a pestle. Whisk together the mustard, sugar, vinegar, soy sauce, sesame oil, safflower oil, peppercorns, ginger and garlic. Toss the vegetables with the dressing and serve at once.

Bean Sprouts in a Sesame Vinaigrette

Serves 8
as a
side dish

Working
time: about
10 minutes

Total time:
about
25 minutes

Calories
50

Protein
2g

Cholesterol
0mg

Total fat
3g

Saturated fat
0g

Sodium
80mg

2 tbsp	Chinese black vinegar or balsamic vinegar	2 tbsp
1 tbsp	low-sodium soy sauce or shoyu	1 tbsp
1 tbsp	safflower oil	1 tbsp
1 tsp	dark sesame oil	1 tsp

1½ tsp	sugar	1½ tsp
500 g	fresh mung bean sprouts	1 lb
1 tbsp	sesame seeds	1 tbsp
1	spring onion, trimmed, finely chopped	1

Bring 3 litres (5 pints) of water to the boil in a large pan. While the water is heating, combine the vinegar, soy sauce, safflower oil, sesame oil and sugar in a small bowl.

Immerse the bean sprouts in the boiling water; stir them once and drain them immediately. Refresh the sprouts under cold running water, then transfer them to a bowl lined with a clean cloth; the cloth will absorb the water. Refrigerate for at least 10 minutes.

Remove the cloth, leaving the sprouts in the bowl. Pour the dressing over the sprouts and toss the salad well. Chill the salad for 5 minutes more and toss it once again. Sprinkle the sesame seeds and chopped spring onion over the top, and serve at once.

Potpourri of Vegetables Bathed in Balsamic Vinegar

Serves 8
as a
first course

Working
time: about
40 minutes

Total time:
about
50 minutes

Calories
80
Protein
3g
Cholesterol
0mg
Total fat
4g
Saturated fat
1g
Sodium
135mg

2½ tbsp	virgin olive oil	2½ tbsp
3	shallots, thinly sliced	3
1	bunch beet greens with stems, washed and thinly sliced (about 125 g/4 oz)	1
1	garlic clove, finely chopped	1
6 tbsp	balsamic vinegar	6 tbsp
2	carrots, halved lengthwise and sliced diagonally into 1 cm (½ inch) pieces	2

2	small turnips, peeled and cut into bâtonnets	2
150 g	small broccoli florets	5 oz
250 g	courgettes, halved lengthwise and sliced diagonally into 1 cm (½ inch) pieces	8 oz
125 g	small yellow squash or courgettes, halved lengthwise and sliced diagonally into 1 cm (½ inch) pieces	4 oz
¼ tsp	salt	¼ tsp
	freshly ground black pepper	

Pour 3 litres (5 pints) of water into a large pan; add 1 tsp of salt and bring the water to the boil.

In the meantime, heat 1½ tbsp of the oil in a large, heavy frying pan set over medium heat. Add the shallots and garlic, and cook them for 2 minutes. Stir in the beet greens and their stems, the ¼ tsp of salt and some pepper. Cook the mixture, stirring frequently, for 7 mins. Pour the vinegar over the mixture, stir well, and remove the pan from the heat.

Put the carrots into the boiling water and cook them for 1 min. Add the turnips and broccoli to the carrots in the pan, and cook them for 2 mins. Add the courgettes and yellow squash to the pan, and cook all the vegetables together for 30 secs more. Immediately drain the vegetables and refresh them under cold running water; when they are cool, drain them on paper towels.

Transfer the vegetables to a bowl and pour the contents of the frying pan over them. Dribble the remaining tbsp of the oil over the top, add a liberal grinding of pepper, and toss the salad well. Chill for at least 10 mins. Toss it once more before presenting it at the table.

Tomato Fans with Basil, Prosciutto and Provolone

Serves 4
as a first
course or
side dish

Working
time: about
20 minutes

Totat time:
about
35 minutes

Calories
105
Protein
5g
Cholesterol
11mg
Total fat
7g
Saturated fat
2g
Sodium
280mg

2	large ripe tomatoes, cored	2
¼ tsp	sugar	¼ tsp
⅛ tsp	sugar freshly ground black pepper	⅛ tsp
2 tbsp	red wine vinegar	2 tbsp
1	shallot, finely chopped	1
1 tbsp	virgin olive oil	1 tbsp
2	garlic cloves, crushed	2

45 g	thinly sliced prosciutto, julienned	1½ oz
30 g	provolone cheese, thinly sliced and julienned	1 oz
2 tbsp	thinly sliced fresh basil leaves	2 tbsp
1	round lettuce (about 125 g/4 oz), washed and dried	1

Halve the tomatoes from top to bottom, then, with the cut side down, thinly slice each half, and set it aside intact. Transfer the sliced halves to a plate. Gently fan out each half. Sprinkle the tomatoes with the sugar, salt and a generous grinding of black pepper, then dribble 1 tablespoon of the wine vinegar over them. Refrigerate the tomato fans for about 10 minutes.

Meanwhile, prepare the dressing. Put the fine chopped shallot and the remaining tablespoon of vinegar into a bowl. Whisk in the oil. Add the garlic prosciutto, provolone cheese, basil and some more pepper, and stir the mixture to combine it; set it aside.

Arrange the lettuce on a serving platter and place the tomato fans on the leaves. Remove the garlic cloves from the dressing and spoon a quarter of it on each tomato fan. Serve the salad immediately.

Baby Leeks in Caper-Cream Vinaigrette

Serves 6 as a first course		Calories 190
Working time: about 20 minutes		Protein 2g
		Cholesterol 3mg
		Total fat 4g
Total time: about 45 minutes		Saturated fat 1g
		Sodium 200mg

12	baby leeks (about 750 g/1½ lb), trimmed, green tops cut to within 5 cm (2 inches) of the white part	**12**
2 tsp	fresh thyme, or ½ tsp dried thyme	**2 tsp**
2	shallots, finely chopped	**2**
⅛ tsp	salt	**⅛ tsp**
	freshly ground black pepper	

1 tbsp	fresh lemon juice	**1 tbsp**
1 tbsp	red wine vinegar	**1 tbsp**
1 tsp	capers, rinsed and chopped	**1 tsp**
1 tbsp	virgin olive oil	**1 tbsp**
2 tbsp	single cream	**2 tbsp**
2 tbsp	chopped sweet red pepper	**2 tbsp**
1	garlic clove, very finely chopped	**1**

Wash each leek to remove the grit: without splitting the leek or detaching any leaves, gently prize apart the leaves and run cold water between them to force out the dirt. Shake the excess water from the leaves and repeat the washing process. Arrange the leeks in a pan large enough to hold them in a single layer. Pour in just enough water to cover the leeks; add the thyme, half of the shallots, ⅛ teaspoon of the salt and a lavish grinding of pepper. Poach the leeks over medium-low heat for 10 minutes. Gently turn the leeks over, and continue poaching them until they are tender–about 10 minutes

more. Transfer the leeks to a plate lined with a double thickness of paper towels. Refrigerate the leeks until they are cool–at least 20 minutes.

About 10 minutes before the leeks are sufficiently chilled, combine the remaining shallots in a small bowl with the lemon juice, vinegar, capers, the remaining ⅛ teaspoon of salt and some more pepper. Let the vinaigrette stand for 5 minutes, then whisk in the oil, cream, red pepper and garlic.

Transfer the cooled leeks to a serving dish. Pour the vinaigrette over the leeks and serve them at once.

Dandelion Greens with Potato and Bacon

Serve 4
as a
first course

Working
time: about
30 minutes

Total time:
about
45 minutes

Calories
130
Protein
5g
Cholesterol
9mg
Total fat
6g
Saturated fat
1g
Sodium
265mg

1	large waxy potato	1	½ tsp	sugar	½ tsp
1 tbsp	safflower oil	1 tbsp	⅛ tsp	salt	⅛ tsp
45 g	mild back bacon, julienned	1½ oz		freshly ground black pepper	
2	shallots, thinly sliced	2	250 g	dandelion greens, washed	8 oz
2 tbsp	red wine vinegar	2 tbsp		and dried	
4 tbsp	unsalted chicken stock	4 tbsp			

Boil the potato until it is barely tender – about 15 minutes. Remove the potato from the water and set it aside until it is cool enough to handle. Peel the potato and cut it into small dice.

Heat the safflower oil in a heavy frying pan over medium-high heat. Add the bacon and shallots, and sauté them until the bacon begins to brown – 4 to 5 minutes. Add the diced potato

and continue sautéing until the potato pieces begin to brown too – about 3 minutes more.

Stir in the vinegar and cook the mixture for 2 minutes. Add the stock, sugar, salt and some pepper; cook the mixture, stirring often, until the liquid is reduced by half – about 3 minutes.

Pour the contents of the pan over the dandelion greens and toss well; serve the salad immediately.

Moulded Leek Salads

Serves 4 as a first course		Calories 80
Working time: about 30 minutes		Protein 6g
		Cholesterol 2mg
Total time: about 2 hours and 30 minutes		Total fat 1g
		Saturated fat 0g
		Sodium 80mg

350 g	leeks, trimmed, split, washed, thoroughly to remove all grit, and sliced crosswise into 5 mm (¼ inch) thick pieces	12 oz
¼ litre	cold unsalted chicken stock	8 fl oz
1 tbsp	fresh lemon juice	1 tbsp
1 tbsp	powdered gelatine	1 tbsp

12.5 cl	plain low-fat yogurt	4 fl oz
½ tbsp	Dijon mustard	½ tbsp
4 tbsp	finely chopped parsley	4 tbsp
1 tbsp	finely cut fresh chives	1 tbsp
	freshly ground black pepper	
	watercress sprigs for garnish	

Add the leeks to 2 litres (3½ pints) of water boiling in a pan. Return the water to the boil and cook the leeks until they are tender – about 2 minutes. Drain the leeks thoroughly and allow them to cool.

In a bowl, combine half of the stock with the lemon juice. Sprinkle the gelatine on top of the liquid and allow it to soften. Meanwhile, heat the remaining stock in a small saucepan over low heat. Pour the gelatine mixture into the pan, then stir gently until the gelatine disolves. Return the gelatine mixture to the bowl and set the bowl in a larger vessel filled with ice cubes. Whisk in the yogurt and mustard. Chill the

mixture, stirring it from time to time. When it begins to set – after about 20 minutes – fold in the leeks, parsley, chives and some pepper.

Rinse four 12.5cl (4 fl oz) ramekins with cold water. Shake the ramekins dry, leaving a few drops of water clinging inside. Divide the leek mixture evenly among the ramekins, then chill them until the mixture is firm – about 2 hours.

To serve the moulded salads, run the tip of a knife around the inside of each ramekin. Dip the bottoms of the ramekins in hot water for about 15 seconds, then unmould the salads on to individual plates. Garnish each one with a few sprigs of watercress and serve at once.

Batavian Endive Chiffonade with Peppers

Serves 6
as a
side dish

Working
time: about
20 minutes

Total time:
about
45 minutes

Calories
55
Protein
2g
Cholesterol
0mg
Total fat
4g
Saturated fat
1g
Sodium
125mg

12.5 cl	unsalted veal or chicken stock	**4 fl oz**
2	sweet black peppers, seeded and deribbed, one coarsely chopped, the other very thinly sliced	**2**
1	dried hot red chili pepper, seeded and crushed	**1**
1	shallot, coarsely chopped	**1**
1½ tbsp	red wine vinegar	**1½ tbsp**
¾ tsp	sugar	**¾ tsp**
¼ tsp	salt	**¼ tsp**
	freshly ground black peppers	
1½ tbsp	virgin olive oil	**1½ tbsp**
1 tbsp	fresh lime juice	**1 tbsp**
1	large Batavian endive, (about 750 g/½ lb) trimmed, cut in half through core	**1**

In a small frying pan, combine the stock, the chopped sweet pepper, chilli pepper, shallot, vinegar, sugar, salt and some pepper. Simmer over low heat, stirring frequently, until only about 3 tablespoons of liquid remain – 7 to 10 minutes.

Transfer the contents of the pan to a blender. Add the oil and lime juice and purée the mixture to obtain a smooth dressing, Transfer the dressing to a large bowl; immediately add the sliced sweet pepper. Refrigerate the dressing until it is cool – about 15 minutes.

Lay an endive half on a work surface cut side down and slice it into chiffonade. Repeat the process with the other half. Toss the chiffonade with the dressing and serve the salad at once.

Gingery Cauliflower Salad

Serves 4 as a first course or side dish	
Working time: about 20 minutes	
Total time: about 45 minutes	

Calories	60
Protein	1g
Cholesterol	0mg
Total fat	4g
Saturated fat	0g
Sodium	150mg

1	cauliflower, trimmed and cut into florets	1
2.5 cm	piece fresh ginger root, peeled and julienned	1 inch
1	carrot, julienned	1
2 tbsp	white vinegar	2 tbsp
½ tsp	sugar	½ tsp
¼ tsp	salt	¼ tsp
⅛ tsp	cayenne pepper	⅛ tsp
1 tbsp	safflower oil	1 tbsp
¼ tsp	dark sesame oil	¼ tsp
1	spring onion, trimmed, green part julienned and soaked in iced water, white parts sliced diagonally into thin ovals	1

Mound the cauliflower florets on a heatproof plate to resemble a whole head of cauliflower. Scatter the ginger and carrot julienne over the cauliflower.

Combine the vinegar, sugar, salt and cayenne pepper in a small bowl. Whisk in the safflower oil and pour the dressing over the cauliflower.

Pour enough water into a large pan to fill it about 2.5 cm (1 inch) deep. Stand two or three small heat-proof bowls in the water and set the plate with the cauliflower on top of the bowls. Cover the pan, bring the water to the boil and steam the cauliflower until it can be easily pierced with a knife – 15 to 20 minutes.

Remove the lid and let the steam dissipate. Lift the plate out of the pan and let the cauliflower stand until it cools to room temperature. Dribble the sesame oil over the cauliflower and scatter the green and white spring onion on top. Serve the salad at room temperature or chilled.

Sprouted Three-Bean Salad

Serves 4
as a
side dish

Working
time: about
15 minutes

Total time:
about
1 hour and
25 minutes
(includes
chilling)

Calories
80

Protein
3g

Cholesterol
0mg

Total fat
4g

Saturated fat
0g

Sodium
180mg

45 g	sweet green pepper, chopped	1½ oz
30 g	red onion, thinly sliced	1 oz
1	garlic clove, finely chopped	1
2 tbsp	chopped fresh basil, or 2 tsp dried basil	2 tbsp
2 tbsp	white vinegar	2 tbsp
2 tsp	sugar	2 tsp

¼ tsp	salt	¼ tsp
	freshly ground black pepper	
60 g	sprouted chick-peas	2 oz
60 g	sprouted pinto beans	2 oz
75 g	sprouted mung beans	2½ oz
1 tbsp	safflower oil	1 tbsp
1	lettuce, washed and dried	1

Bring two pans of water to the boil.

In a small bowl, combine the green pepper, onion, garlic, basil, vinegar, sugar, salt and some pepper. Set the mixture aside for at least 5 minutes.

Combine the sprouted chick-peas and pinto beans, and blanch them in one of your pans of boiling water until they are tender – 5 to 7 minutes. Blanch the sprouted mung beans in the other pan until they too are tender – 2 to 3 minutes. Drain all of the beans, rinse them under cold running water, drain again, and toss them together in a bowl.

Add the oil to the vinegar mixture and stir it in well. Pour the dressing over the sprouted beans and stir to coat them. Chill the salad for 1 hour in the refrigerator before serving it on a bed of lettuce.

Sweet Potato Salad with Peanuts

Serves 8
as a
side dish

Working
time: about
30 minutes

Total time:
about
1 hour and
30 minutes

Calories
150
Protein
4g
Cholesterol
0mg
Total fat
4g
Saturated fat
0g
Sodium
140mg

750 g	sweet potatoes, peeled, halved lengthwise and cut into 5 mm (¼ inch) thick slices	1½ lb	
250 g	French beans, trimmed and cut in half	8 oz	
3	spring onions, trimmed and thinly sliced	3	
750 g	Chinese cabbage, sliced into chiffonade	1½ lb	
2tbsp	coarsely chopped dry-roasted unsalted peanuts	2 tbsp	

Ginger Dressing

4 tbsp	rice vinegar	4 tbsp
1 tbsp	low-sodium soy sauce or shoyu	1 tbsp
1 tbsp	safflower oil	1 tbsp
1 tsp	dark sesame oil	1 tsp
1	hot green chili pepper, seeded, deribbed, and finely chopped	1
1 tbsp	finely chopped fresh ginger root	1 tbsp
1	garlic clove, finely chopped	1
	freshly ground black pepper	

To cook the sweet potatoes, pour enough water into a saucepan to fill it about 2.5 cm (1 inch) deep. Set a steamer in the pan and bring the water to the boil. Put the sweet potatoes into the steamer, cover the pan tightly, and steam the sweet potatoes until they are just tender – about 10 minutes. Transfer the sweet potatoes to a large bowl and set them aside.

Steam the beans until they are cooked but still crisp – about 4 minutes. Refresh the beans under running water to preserve their colour, then add them to the bowl with the sweet potatoes.

While the beans are cooking, prepare the dressing: combine the vinegar and soy sauce in a small bowl. Whisk in the oils, then the chili pepper, ginger, garlic and some black pepper.

Pour all but 2 tablespoons of the dressing over the sweet potatoes and beans; add the spring onions and toss well. Chill the vegetables for at least 1 hour.

To serve the salad, toss the cabbage with the remaining 2 tablespoons of dressing and transfer it to a serving plate. Mound the chilled vegetables on top and scatter the peanuts over all.

Endive Salad with Orange and Rosemary

Serves 6
as a
first course
or a
side dish

Working
(and total)
time: about
25 minutes

Calories
70
Protein
2g
Cholesterol
0mg
Total fat
4g
Saturated fat
1g
Sodium
105mg

1	garlic clove, cut in half	1
1	head of curly endive, washed and dried	1
3	small heads of chicory, washed, dried and sliced crosswise into 1 cm (½ inch) wide strips	3
1	navel orange	1
1	small red onion, thinly sliced	1

1 tbsp	chopped fresh rosemary, or 1 tsp dried rosemary, crumbled	1 tbsp
⅛ tsp	salt	⅛ tsp
2 tbsp	sherry vinegar or red wine vinegar	2 tbsp
1 tbsp	grainy mustard	1 tbsp
1½ tbsp	virgin olive oil	1½ tbsp

Rub the inside of a salad bowl with the cut surfaces of the garlic clove. Put the endive and chicory into the bowl. Working over a bowl to catch the juice, cut away the peel, white pith and outer membrane from the flesh of the orange. To separate the segments from the membranes, slice down to the core with a sharp knife on either side of each segment and set the segments aside. Cut each segment in thirds and add them

to the bowl along with the onion and Rosemary.

In a small bowl, whisk together the salt, reserved orange juice, vinegar and mustard. Whisking constantly, pour in the oil in a thin, steady stream to create an emulsified dressing. Pour the dressing over the contents of the salad bowl; toss the salad thoroughly and serve it at once.

Broccoli and Chinese Salad with Vinegar Dressing

Serves 8 as a side dish

Working (and total) time: about 25 minutes

Calories 40
Protein 2g
Cholesterol 0mg
Total fat 2g
Saturated fat 0g
Sodium 120mg

2	broccoli stalks, florets separated from stems, peeled and sliced diagonally	2
1	daikon radish (mooli)	1
300 g	Chinese cabbage, sliced into 1 cm (½ inch) pieces	10 oz
1 tbsp	safflower oil	1 tbsp
¼ tsp	dark sesame oil	¼ tsp

	Black Vinegar Dressing	
½ litre	unsalted chicken stock	16 fl oz
4	thin slices peeled fresh ginger root	4
1 tsp	Sichuan peppercorns	1 tsp
¼ tsp	sugar	¼ tsp
2 tbsp	Chinese black vinegar or balsamic vinegar	2 tbsp
1 tbsp	low-sodium soy sauce or shoyu	1 tbsp

To make the dressing, first pour the stock into a small pan set over medium-high heat. Add the ginger, peppercorns and sugar, and bring to the boil. Cook the mixture until it is reduced to about 12.5 cl (4 fl oz) – 10 to 12 minutes.

While the stock is reducing, cook the broccoli. Pour enough water into a saucepan to fill it about 2.5 cm (1 inch) deep. Set a vegetable steamer in the water and add the broccoli florets and stems. Cover the pan tightly, bring the water to the boil, and steam the broccoli until it is barely tender – about 2 minutes. Transfer the broccoli to a bowl and refrigerate it until serving time.

Remove the reduced stock from the heat and

let it cool. Stir in the vinegar and soy sauce, then strain the dressing into a small bowl.

Slice the daikon radish into 5 cm (2 inch) lengths. Stand one of the pieces on end; using a small, sharp knife, cut down the sides to remove the peel, giving the radish five sides. Repeat the process to fashion the remaining radish pieces. Thinly slice the pieces; keep them in iced water until serving time.

Drain the radish, dry with paper towels, and transfer to a large bowl along with the broccoli and cabbage. Combine the safflower and sesame oil; dribble the oils over the vegetables, toss well and serve. Pass the dressing separately.

Sweet Potato Salad with Curried Yogurt Dressing

Serves 6
as a
side dish

Working
time: about
30 minutes

Total time:
about
2 hours
(includes
chilling)

Calories
120
Protein
3g
Cholesterol
2mg
Total fat
1g
Saturated fat
0g
Sodium
60mg

	Yogurt Dressing	
2 tbsp	cream sherry	2 tbsp
2	garlic cloves, finely chopped	2
1½ tsp	Dijon mustard	1½ tsp
12.5 cl	plain low-fat yogurt	4 fl oz
1 tbsp	soured cream	1 tbsp
⅛ tsp	white pepper	⅛ tsp

500 g	sweet potatoes	1 lb
4	sticks celery, thinly sliced	4
3	spring onions, trimmed and thinly sliced	3
12.5 cl	yogurt dressing mixed with 1½ tsp curry powder	4 fl oz
1 tbsp	each finely cut chives and chopped parsley, or 2 tbsp chopped parsley	1 tbsp

To make the yogurt dressing, put the sherry and garlic into a small saucepan. Bring the mixture to a simmer over medium heat and cook it until nearly all the liquid has evaporated – about 3 minutes. Transfer the mixture to a bowl. Stir in the mustard, then the yogurt, soured cream and pepper. Cover the bowl and store the dressing in the refrigerator; it will keep for two to three days.

Editor's Note: This salad makes a delicious accompaniment to grilled chicken or pork.

Put the sweet potatoes in a deep saucepan and pour in enough water to cover them. Bring the water to the boil and cook the sweet potatoes over medium heat until they are tender – 25 to 30 minutes. Drain the sweet potatoes; when they are cool enough to handle, peel them and cut them into small dice. Put the sweet potatoes in a bowl with the celery and spring onions.

Add the dressing to the vegetables and mix gently. Chill the salad for at least 1 hour. Just before serving, sprinkle the fresh herbs over the top.

Chayote Fans in a Coriander Vinaigrette

Serves 4
as a first
course

Working
time: about
25 minutes

Total time:
about
45 minutes

Calories
60
Protein
1g
Cholesterol
0mg
Total fat
4g
Saturated fat
0g
Sodium
80mg

1	large chayote (about 350 g/12 oz), quartered and seeded	1	½ tsp	sugar		½ tsp
1	lemon	1	⅛ tsp	salt		⅛ tsp
1 tbsp	red wine vinegar	1 tbsp		freshly ground black pepper		
½ tsp	Dijon mustard	½ tsp	1	large dried mild chili pepper, cut in half lengthwise and seeded		1
1 tbsp	safflower oil	1 tbsp				
1 tbsp	chopped fresh coriander	1 tbsp	4	fresh coriander sprigs for garnish		4

Cut a chayote quarter lengthwise into thin slices, leaving the slices attached at the tapered end to form a fan. Repeat the process.

Pour enough water into a saucepan to fill it about 2.5 cm (1 inch) deep. Set a steamer in the pan and bring to the boil. Set the chayote fans in the steamer, cover the pan, and steam the vegetable until it is barely tender – 4 to 5 minutes. Transfer the chayote to a shallow bowl.

Cut the lemon in half. Slice one half into four rounds and reserve the rounds for garnish. Squeeze enough juice from the other half to measure 1 tablespoon and pour it into a small mixing bowl. Add the vinegar and mustard, and whisk in the oil. Season the vinaigrette with the

coriander, sugar, salt and some pepper. Pour the vinaigrette over the chayote fans and chill them.

Meanwhile, place the chili pepper in a small bowl, pour ¼ litre (8 fl oz) of boiling water over it, let it soak for 20 minutes. Remove the chili pepper from its soaking liquid; do not discard the liquid. Put the pepper pieces in a blender along with 4 tablespoons of the soaking liquid. Drain the vinaigrette from the chilled chayote and add it to the pepper pieces and liquid. Purée the dressing and strain it through a fine sieve.

Spoon the dressing on to four individual salad plates. Transfer the chayote fans to the plates and place a sprig of coriander on each fan. Garnish each salad with a lemon round.

Kohlrabi Salad

Serves 6
as a
side dish

Working
(and total)
time: about
40 minutes

Calories
45

Protein
3g

Cholesterol
3mg

Total fat
2g

Saturated fat
0g

Sodium
45mg

500 g	kohlrabies or turnips, peeled and shredded	**1 lb**
4 tbsp	diced pimiento	**4 tbsp**

1 tbsp	fresh lemon juice	**1 tbsp**
12.5 cl	yogurt dressing (recipe, p28)	**4 fl oz**

Pour 2 litres (3½ pints) of cold water into a saucepan. Add the kohlrabi or turnip shreds, bring the water to the boil, then blanch for 2 minutes. Drain them in a colander, refresh them under cold running water, and drain them again. Rid the vegetables of excess moisture by pressing down on them with the back of a large spoon. (Or wrap them in muslin and wring out.)

Transfer the kohlrabi or turnip shreds to a bowl and stir in the pimiento and lemon juice. Pour the dressing over the top, toss the salad well, and serve it at once.

Sautéed Greens with Red Potatoes and Apple

Serves 8 as a side dish		
Working time: about 25 minutes		
Total time: about 1 hour and 25 minutes		

Calories 105		
Protein 2g		
Cholesterol 2mg		
Total fat 3g		
Saturated fat 1g		
Sodium 150mg		

1	large tart apple	1	1½ tbsp	virgin olive oil	1½ tbsp
1 tbsp	fresh lemon juice	1 tbsp	1	shallot, finely chopped	1
500 g	red potatoes, scrubbed and cut into 2 cm (¾ inch) cubes	1 lb	250 g	spinach, spring greens, Swiss chard leaves or young kale, stemmed, washed, torn into 5 cm (2 inch) pieces and dried	8 oz
½ tsp	salt	½ tsp			
	freshly ground black pepper				
1 tbsp	red wine vinegar	1 tbsp	12.5 cl	milk	4 fl oz

Peel, quarter and core the apple, and cut it into 2 cm (¾ inch) pieces. In a small bowl, toss the apple with the lemon juice; set the bowl aside.

Pour ½ litre (16 fl oz) of water into a saucepan. Add the potatoes and salt, and bring the water to the boil. Reduce the heat and simmer the potatoes for 10 minutes. Add the apple to the saucepan and continue cooking the mixture, stirring often so that it does not burn, until only 2 tablespoons of liquid remain – about 10 minutes more.

Combine the wine vinegar and ½ tablespoon of the olive oil in a small bowl. Pour this mixture over the hot potatoes and apple, and set them aside.

Heat the remaining oil in a large, heavy frying pan over medium heat. Cook the shallot in the oil for 1 minute. Add the greens and cook them, stirring frequently, until they are wilted – about 3 minutes. Pour in the milk and continue cooking the mixture until all the liquid has evaporated – 7 to 10 minutes.

Combine the potato mixture, the greens and a generous grinding of pepper in a large bowl. Toss the salad well and refrigerate it for at least 45 minutes. Toss it once more before serving.

Carrot and Orange Salad with Dill

Serves 4
as a
side dish

Working
time: about
10 minutes

Total time:
about
25 minutes

Calories
90

Protein
2g

Cholesterol
0mg

Total fat
0g

Saturated fat
0g

Sodium
50mg

1	large juicy orange	1
600 g	carrots, finely grated	1¼ lb
1 tbsp	red wine vinegar	1 tbsp

12.5 cl	fresh orange juice	4 fl oz
½ tsp	grated orange rind	½ tsp
2 tbsp	fresh dill	2 tbsp

Working over a bowl to catch the juice, cut away the peel, white pith and outer membrane from the orange. To separate the segments from the inner membranes, slice down to the core with a sharp knife on either side of each segment and set the segments aside.

Combine the carrots, vinegar, orange juice and rind in the bowl. Add the orange segments and 1 tablespoon of the dill; gently toss the ingredients. Refrigerate the salad for at least 15 minutes. Shortly before serving, garnish the top with the remaining dill.

Spinach and Sesame Salad

Serves 6
as a
side dish

Working
(and total)
time: about
30 minutes

Calories
60
Protein
4g
Cholesterol
0mg
Total fat
5g
Saturated fat
0g
Sodium
255mg

12.5 cl	unsalted chicken stock	4 fl oz
1 tbsp	sesame seeds	1 tbsp
1 tbsp	tahini (sesame paste)	1 tbsp
1 tsp	dark sesame oil	1 tsp
1½ tbsp	low-sodium soy sauce or shoyu	1½ tbsp
1 tbsp	fresh lemon juice	1 tbsp
1 tsp	finely chopped fresh ginger root	1 tsp

500 g	spinach, washed, stemmed and dried	1 lb
125 g	mushrooms, wiped clean and thinly sliced	4 oz
1	large ripe tomato, sliced into thin wedges	1
⅛ tsp	salt	⅛ tsp
	freshly ground black pepper	

Boil the stock in a small saucepan until only 2 tablespoons remain – about 7 minutes.

While the stock is reducing, toast the sesame seeds in a small, heavy frying pan over medium-low heat until they are golden – about 3 minutes. Set the pan aside.

To prepare the dressing, mix the tahini and sesame oil in a small bowl. Whisk in the reduced stock, the soy sauce, lemon juice and ginger.

Put the spinach and mushrooms into a large bowl. Sprinkle the tomato wedges with the salt and pepper and add them to the bowl. Pour the dressing over the vegetables, grind in some more pepper, and toss well. Scatter the sesame seeds over the salad and serve.

Kale, Pear and Goat Cheese Salad

**Serves 8
as a
first course**

**Working
(and total)
time: about
40 minutes**

**Calories
90
Protein
4g
Cholesterol
5mg
Total fat
4g
Saturated fat
1g
Sodium
200mg**

1½ tbsp	virgin olive oil	1½ tbsp	
500 g	onions, thinly sliced	1 lb	
⅛ tsp	salt	⅛ tsp	
	freshly ground black pepper		
500 g	kale, stemmed and washed, large leaves torn in half	1 lb	
12.5 cl	cider vinegar	4 fl oz	
60 g	thinly sliced pancetta (Italian bacon) or prosciutto, cut into thin strips	2 oz	
1	pear, quartered, cored and thinly sliced lengthwise	1	
60 g	fresh goat cheese, broken into small pieces	2 oz	

Heat 1 tablespoon of the olive oil in a large, heavy frying pan over medium heat. Add the onions and ⅛ teaspoon of salt; cook the onions, scraping the browned bits from the bottom of the pan vigorously and often, until the onions are caramelized – 25 to 30 minutes.

Meanwhile, cook the kale in 3 litres (5 pints) of boiling water for 7 minutes. Drain the kale and refresh it under cold running water. When the kale has cooled thoroughly, mould it into a ball and squeeze out as much liquid as possible.

When the onions are caramelized, stir the vinegar into the pan, scraping up any remaining pan deposits. Continue cooking the mixture until most of the liquid has evaporated – about 5 minutes.

Heat the remaining oil in a smaller frying pan over medium heat. Cook the pancetta or prosciutto in the oil for 1 minute, add it to the onion mixture, then stir in the kale, the sliced pear, the remaining salt and a generous grinding of black pepper. Stir in half of the goat cheese.

Divide the mixture among eight plates; dot the tops of the portions with the remaining cheese and serve the salad immediately.

Potato Salad with Roasted Red Pepper Sauce

Serves 8
as a
side dish

Working
(and total)
time: about
40 minutes

Calories
110
Protein
2g
Cholesterol
0mg
Total fat
4g
Saturated fat
0g
Sodium
70mg

750 g	round red potatoes or other waxy potatoes, scrubbed	**1¼ lb**
2	sweet red peppers	**2**
2	garlic cloves, peeled and crushed	**2**
1 tsp	chopped fresh rosemary, or ½ tsp dried rosemary, crumbled	**1 tsp**
¼ tsp	salt	**¼ tsp**

	cayenne pepper	
2 tbsp	red wine vinegar	**2 tbsp**
2 tbsp	virgin olive oil	**2 tbsp**
175 g	rocket, washed and dried, or 2 bunches watercress, stemmed, washed and dried	**6 oz**

Put the potatoes into a large saucepan and cover them with cold water. Bring the water to the boil and cook the potatoes until they are tender — about 25 minutes. Drain the potatoes and set them aside to cool.

While the potatoes are boiling, roast the peppers about 5 cm (2 inches) below a preheated grill, turning them often, until they are blistered on all sides. Put the peppers into a bowl and cover the bowl with plastic film; the trapped steam will loosen their skins. Peel the peppers,

then seed and derib them. Put the peppers into a food processor or a blender along with the garlic, rosemary, salt and a pinch of cayenne pepper. Purée the mixture to obtain a smooth sauce. With the motor still running, pour in the vinegar, then the oil; continue blending the sauce until it is well combined.

Cut the potatoes in half and then into wedges. Arrange the wedges on a bed of rocket leaves or watercress. Pour some of the sauce over the potatoes and serve the rest alongside.

Broad Bean Salad

Serves 6
as a first
course or
side dish

Working
time: about
40 minutes

Total time:
about
50 minutes

Calories
125
Protein
6g
Cholesterol
3mg
Total fat
3g
Saturated fat
1g
Sodium
95mg

2 tsp	virgin olive oil	2 tsp
1	large onion, thinly sliced	1
1	large garlic clove, finely chopped	½ tsp
1.25 kg	fresh broad beans, shelled and peeled, or 150 g (5 oz) frozen broad beans	2½ lb
30 g	paper-thin slices of prosciutto, julienned	1 oz
1 tbsp	chopped fresh oregano, or 1 tsp dried oregano	1 tbsp

750 g	ripe tomatoes, skinned, seeded coarsely chopped, or 400 g (14 oz) canned tomatoes, chopped, with juice	1½ lb
¼ litre	unsalted chicken stock, or 12.5 cl (4 fl oz) unsalted chicken stock if canned tomatoes are used	8 fl oz
½ tsp	cracked black peppercorns	½ tsp
2 tbsp	balsamic vinegar, or 1½ tbsp red wine vinegar mixed with ½ tsp honey	2 tbsp

Heat the oil in a heavy frying pan over medium heat. Add the onion slices and cook them until they are translucent – 4 to 5 minutes. Stir in the garlic and cook the mixture for 1 minute more. Add the beans, prosciutto, tomatoes, stock, oregano and peppercorns. Bring the liquid to a simmer and cook the mixture until the beans are just tender – 8 to 10 minutes.

Transfer to a bowl and refrigerate. When the salad is cool, pour in the vinegar, toss well and serve at once.

French Bean Salad with Gruyère and Grainy Mustard

Serves 6
as a first
course or
side dish

Working
time: about
15 minutes

Total time:
about
30 minutes

Calories
70

Protein
3g

Cholesterol
8mg

Total fat
5g

Saturated fat
2g

Sodium
120mg

350 g	French beans, trimmed, halved diagonally	12 oz
1	shallot, finely chopped	1
1½ tbsp	grainy mustard, or 1 tbsp Dijon mustard	1½ tbsp

3 tbsp	red wine vinegar	3 tbsp
1 tbsp	virgin olive oil	1 tbsp
⅛ tsp	salt	⅛ tsp
	freshly ground black pepper	
45 g	Gruyère cheese, julienned	1½ oz

Pour enough water into a large saucepan to fill it about 2.5 cm (1 inch) deep. Set a vegetable steamer in the pan and bring the water to the boil. Put the beans into the steamer, cover the pan, and cook the beans until they are just tender – 7 to 8 minutes. Refresh the beans under cold running water; when they are cool, drain them on paper towels.

Mix the shallot, mustard, vinegar, oil, salt and some pepper in a large bowl. Add the cheese and beans, and toss them well. Refrigerate the salad for 10 minutes. Toss it once again just before serving.

Broccoli Salad with Oven-Roasted Mushrooms

Serves 8
as a first
course or
side dish

Working
(and total)
time: about
1 hour and
15 minutes

Calories
105

Protein
6g

Cholesterol
0mg

Total fat
4g

Saturated fat
0g

Sodium
150mg

1 kg	mushrooms, wiped clean, stems trimmed	2 lb	1	red or green-leaf lettuce, washed and dried	1
4	large shallots, thinly sliced lengthwise	4		**Mustard Dressing**	
6 tbsp	fresh lemon juice	6 tbsp	2 tbsp	grainy mustard	2 tbsp
2½ tbsp	fresh thyme, or 2 tsp dried thyme	2½ tbsp	3 tbsp	balsamic vinegar, or 2½ tbsp red wine vinegar mixed with 1 tsp honey	3 tbsp
¼ tsp	salt	¼ tsp	1 tbsp	chopped parsley	1 tbsp
	freshly ground black pepper		2 tsp	chopped fresh oregano, or ½ tsp dried oregano	2 tsp
1 tbsp	safflower oil	1 tbsp		freshly ground black pepper	
1.25 kg	broccoli, stemmed and cut into florets	2½ lb	1 tbsp	safflower oil	1 tbsp

Preheat the oven to 230°C (450°F or Mark 8). Put the mushrooms in a baking dish. Add the shallots, lemon juice, thyme, salt, some pepper and the tablespoon of oil; toss the mixture to coat the mushrooms. Spread in a single layer, then roast them until they are tender and most of the liquid has evaporated – 20 to 25 minutes. Remove from the oven and keep the dish warm.

While the mushrooms are cooking, make the dressing. Combine the mustard, vinegar, parsley, oregano and some pepper in a small bowl.

Whisking vigorously, pour in the tbsp of oil in a thin, steady stream. Whisk until the dressing is well combined; set the dressing aside.

Pour water into a saucepan to fill it about 2.5 cm (1 inch) deep. Set a steamer in the pan and bring to the boil. Put the broccoli into the steamer, cover the pan, and steam until it is tender but still crisp – about 4 minutes. Add to the dish with the mushrooms. Pour the dressing over and toss the salad well. Arrange on a bed of the lettuce leaves; serve warm or chilled.

Mango and Grape with Cardamom-Yogurt Dressing

Serves 8 as a first course or side dish

Working (and total) time: about 50 minutes

Calories
110
Protein
4g
Cholesterol
2mg
Total fat
1g
Saturated fat
0g
Sodium
30mg

4	cardamom pods, or ¼ tsp ground cardamom	4	1	cos lettuce, washed and dried	1
1 tsp	finely grated fresh ginger root	1 tsp	3	firm mangoes, peeled and cut into 1 cm (½ inch) cubes	3
¼ litre	plain low-fat yogurt	8 fl oz	350 g	seedless red or green grapes, or a mixture of both, halved	12 oz
2 tbsp	fresh orange juice	2 tbsp	1 tbsp	coarsely chopped unsalted pistachio nuts	1 tbsp
1 tbsp	honey	1 tbsp			
2 tbsp	dried skimmed milk	2 tbsp			

Remove the cardamom seeds from their pods and grind them with a mortar and pestle. Place the ground spice in a bowl and add the ginger, yogurt, orange juice, honey and dried milk. Whisk the ingredients together. Let the dressing stand at room temperature for at least 20 minutes to thicken it and allow the different flavours to meld.

To assemble the salad, arrange the lettuce leaves on individual plates and spoon the mango and grapes on to the lettuce. Pour the dressing over each salad and sprinkle the chopped pistachios on top. Serve at once.

Midsummer Melon Salad with Almond Oil

Serves 6
as a first
course or
side dish

Working
time: about
30 minutes

Total time:
about
1 hour and
30 minutes
(includes
chilling)

Calories
120

Protein
2g

Cholesterol
0mg

Total fat
3g

Saturated fat
0g

Sodium
70mg

1	large Charentais melon, seeded, the flesh cut into 4 cm (1½ inch) long pieces	1	1 tbsp	coarsely chopped fresh ginger root	1 tbsp
½	Gallia or Ogen melon, seeded, the flesh cut into 4 cm (1½ inch) long pieces	½	⅛ tsp	salt	⅛ tsp
½	honeydew melon, seeded, the flesh cut into 4 cm (1½ inch) long pieces	½		freshly ground black pepper	
			4 tbsp	rice vinegar	4 tbsp
			1 tbsp	almond or walnut oil	1 tbsp

Combine all the melon pieces in a bowl.

Using a mortar and pestle, crush the chopped fresh ginger with the salt and a generous grinding of pepper. Pour in the rice vinegar and continue crushing to extract as much juice from the ginger as possible. Working over the bowl containing the melon, strain the ginger-vinegar mixture through several layers of muslin; twist the corners of the muslin in your hands and squeeze hard so as to extract the last few drops of liquid from the ginger.

Dribble the almond or walnut oil over the melon pieces and gently toss them to disribute the dressing. Serve the salad well chilled.

Fresh Fruit Salad with Cranberry Dressing

Serves 8
as a
side dish

Working
time: about
15 minutes

Total time:
about
25 minutes

Calories
105
Protein
1g
Cholesterol
0mg
Total fat
4g
Saturated fat
0g
Sodium
40mg

45 g	fresh cranberries, or frozen cranberries, thawed	1½ oz	4	tart red apples, cored and cut into cubes	4
4 tbsp	white vinegar	4 tbsp	325 g	seedless green grapes, halved	11 oz
1 tbsp	honey	1 tbsp	1	lemon, juice only	1
½ tbsp	finely chopped shallot	½ tbsp	1	large round lettuce, washed and dried	1
⅛ tsp	salt	⅛ tsp			
2 tbsp	safflower oil	2 tbsp			

Put the cranberries, vinegar and honey in a small saucepan and bring the mixture to the boil. Reduce the heat to medium low and simmer the mixture until the cranberries are quite soft and the juice has thickened – about 5 minutes. Purée the mixture, then strain it through a fine sieve. Set the cranberry purée aside and allow it to cool to room temperature.

Whisk the shallot, salt and oil into the cooled purée.

Toss the apples and grapes with the lemon juice. Arrange the lettuce leaves on eight individual plates and spoon the fruit on to the leaves. Ladle the purée evenly over the salad.

Brown Rice and Mango Salad

Serves 8
as a
side dish

Working
time: about
20 minutes

Total time:
about
1 hour and
30 minutes

Calories
140
Protein
2g
Cholesterol
0mg
Total fat
4g
Saturated fat
0g
Sodium
70mg

185 g	brown rice	6½ oz	1	small shallot, finely chopped	1
4 tbsp	red wine vinegar	4 tbsp	¼ tsp	ground cardamom	¼ tsp
¼ tsp	salt	¼ tsp		mace	
2 tbsp	safflower oil	2 tbsp		cayenne pepper	
1	sweet green pepper, seeded and deribbed	1	1	ripe mango, peeled and diced	1

Bring 1.5 litres (2½ pints) of water to the boil in a large saucepan. Stir in the rice, reduce the heat and simmer, uncovered, until tender – about 35 minutes. Drain the rice and put it in a serving bowl. Stir in the vinegar and salt, and allow the mixture to cool to room temperature – about 30 minutes.

When the rice is cool, stir in the oil, pepper, shallot, cardamom and a pinch each of mace and cayenne pepper. Add the mango pieces and stir them in gently so that they retain their shape. Cover the salad; to allow the flavours to meld, let the salad stand, unrefrigerated, for about 30 minutes before serving.

Apricots and Water Chestnuts in Wild Rice

Serves 8
as a
side dish

Working
time: about
30 minutes

Total time:
about
1 hour

Calories
130
Protein
4g
Cholesterol
0mg
Total fat
0g
Saturated fat
0g
Sodium
75mg

160 g	wild rice	5¼ oz		**Spicy Lemon Dressing**	
125 g	dried apricots, cut into 1 cm (½ inch) pieces	4 oz	2 tbsp	fresh lemon juice	2 tbsp
175 g	fresh water chestnuts, peeled, and quartered, or 250 g (8 oz) canned whole peeled water chestnuts, drained, rinsed and quartered	6 oz	1 tbsp	red wine vinegar	1 tbsp
			⅛ tsp	ground ginger	⅛ tsp
			⅛ tsp	cinnamon ground cloves	⅛ tsp
2 tbsp	chopped parsley	2 tbsp	¼ tsp	salt freshly ground black pepper	¼ tsp

Bring 1.5 litres (2½ pints) of water to the boil in a saucepan. Stir in the wild rice, reduce the heat, and simmer the rice, uncovered, until it is tender but still chewy – approximately 45 minutes.

While the rice cooks, prepare the apricots and dressing: put the apricots into a small bowl and pour in enough hot water to cover them by about 2.5 cm (1 inch). Soak the apricots for 20 minutes to soften them. Drain the apricots, reserving 4 tablespoons of their soaking liquid, and set them aside.

Pour the reserved apricot-soaking liquid into a small bowl. Add the lemon juice, vinegar, ginger, cinnamon, a pinch of cloves, the salt and some pepper; whisk the mixture vigorously until it is thoroughly combined.

When the rice finishes cooking, drain and rinse it, and transfer it to a serving bowl. Pour the dressing over the rice, then add the apricots, water chestnuts and the parsley; toss the ingredients well and serve the salad at room temperature.

Wheat Berry and Orange Salad

Serves 6
as a first
course or
side dish

Working
time: about
45 minutes

Total time:
about
2 hours

Calories
280
Protein
6g
Cholesterol
0mg
Total fat
5g
Saturated fat
1g
Sodium
125mg

190 g	wheat berries	**6½ oz**
¼ tsp	salt	**¼ tsp**
6	large sweet oranges (about 250 g/8 oz each)	**6**
75 g	raisins	**2½ oz**
2 tsp	sherry vinegar or red wine vinegar	**2 tsp**
1 tbsp	grainy mustard	**1 tbsp**
2 tbsp	virgin olive oil	**2 tbsp**
	freshly ground black pepper	
1 tsp	grated orange rind	**1 tsp**
45 g	raisins	**1½ oz**
45 g	spring onions, thinly sliced	**1½ oz**
4 tbsp	thinly sliced mint leaves	**4 tbsp**
6	mint sprigs for garnish	**6**

Bring ¼ litre (16 fl oz) of water to the boil in a pan. Stir in the wheat berries and salt. Reduce the heat to low, cover the pan, and simmer the kernels until they are tender – 1½ to 2 hours. If the wheat berries absorb all the water before they finish cooking, pour in more water, 4 tablespoons at a time, to keep the kernels from burning. Drain, and set aside to cool.

While the wheat berries are cooking, hollow out the oranges. Using your fingers, a knife or a spoon, separate 90 g (3 oz) of the orange flesh from the pulp; coarsely chop the flesh and set it aside. Squeeze the juice from the remaining pulp and reserve 12.5 cl (4 fl oz) of it. (Save the

rest of the juice for another use.) Combine the measured juice in a small bowl with the raisins; let the raisins soak for 15 minutes.

To prepare the dressing, transfer 2 tablespoons or the raisin-soaked liquid to a large bowl. Add the vinegar and mustard. Slowly whisk in the oil, then season the dressing with some pepper.

Add to the bowl the drained wheat berries, chopped orange flesh, orange rind, raisins with their remaining soaking liquid, spring onion and sliced mint. Stir to combine the ingredients, then spoon the mixture into orange shells. Replace the orange tops and garnish each shell with a sprig of mint before serving.

Burghul Salad with Raisins and Courgettes

Serves 12
as a
side dish

Working
time: about
20 minutes

Total time:
about
1 hour and
30 minutes

Calories
125

Protein
4g

Cholesterol
0mg

Total fat
1g

Saturated fat
0g

Sodium
5mg

325 g	burghul	**11 oz**
2	courgettes, each cut crosswise into 5 mm (¼ inch) slices, each slice cut into eight wedges	**2**
5	spring onions, trimmed and sliced	**5**
12.5 cl	red wine vinegar	**4 fl oz**
1	sweet yellow pepper, seeded, deribbed and cut into 1 cm (½ inch) squares	**1**
4 tbsp	raisins	**4 tbsp**
⅛ tsp	cayenne pepper	**⅛ tsp**
⅛ tsp	ground cardamon	**⅛ tsp**
⅛ tsp	ground coriander	**⅛ tsp**
	ground cloves	
	ground ginger	
	ground mace	

Put the burghul into a heatproof bowl and pour ¾ litre (1¼ pints) of boiling water over it. Cover the bowl and set it aside for 30 minutes.

At the end of the soaking period, mix in the courgettes, spring onions, vinegar, yellow pepper, raisins, cayenne pepper, cardamom, coriander, and a pinch each of cloves, ginger and mace. Let the salad stand for at least 30 minutes before serving it either chilled or at room temperature.

Red Lentils with White Rice and Pearl Onions

Serves 6
as a
side dish

Working
time: about
15 minutes

Total time:
about
30 minutes

Calories
200

Protein
8g

Cholesterol
0mg

Total fat
3g

Saturated fat
0g

Sodium
20mg

190 g	red lentils, picked over	6½ oz
90 g	long-grain rice	3 oz
2 tbsp	sugar	2 tbsp
4 tbsp	raspberry vinegar	4 tbsp
6 tbsp	unsalted chicken stock	6 tbsp

175 g	pearl onions, blanched for	6 oz
	2 minutes in boiling water	2
	and peeled	
1 tsp	Dijon mustard	1 tsp
	freshly ground black pepper	
1 tbsp	safflower oil	1 tbsp

Bring the lentils and ¾ litre (1¼ pints) of water to the boil in a small saucepan over medium-high heat. Reduce the heat and simmer the lentils until they are tender – 15 to 20 minutes. Avoid overcooking or the lentils will lose much of their colour. Drain the lentils and put them into a large bowl.

Start cooking the rice while the lentils are simmering. Bring the rice and ¼ litre (8 fl oz) of water to the boil in a small saucepan over medium-high heat. Reduce the heat, cover the saucepan, and simmer the rice until the liquid has been absorbed and the rice is tender – about 20 minutes. Add the rice to the lentils.

While the rice is cooking, sprinkle the sugar into a sauté pan and set it over medium heat.

Cook the sugar until it liquefies and starts to caramelize. Pour in 3 tablespoons of the vinegar and 4 tablespoons of the chicken stock. As the liquid comes to a simmer, stir it to incorporate the caramelized sugar, then add the pearl onions. Cook the onions, stirring from time to time, until they are glazed and nearly all the liquid in the pan has evaporated. Add the glazed onions to the lentils and rice in the bowl.

To prepare the dressing, combine the remaining raspberry vinegar and chicken stock, the mustard and some pepper in a small bowl. Whisk in the oil, then pour the vinaigrette over the lentil and rice mixture, and toss well. This salad is best served cold.

Aubergine, Cucumber and White Bean Salad

<table>
<tr><td>Serves 12
as a
side dish

Working
time: about
30 minutes

Total time:
about
3 hours
(includes
soaking and
chilling)</td><td></td><td>Calories
120
Protein
7g
Cholesterol
0mg
Total fat
1g
Saturated fat
0g
Sodium
95mg</td></tr>
</table>

500 g	dried haricot beans, picked over	1 lb		1 tsp	chopped fresh sage, or ¼ tsp dried sage, crushed	1 tsp
350 g	aubergine, cut into 1 cm (½ inch) cubes	12 oz		1	garlic clove, finely chopped	1
1	onion, chopped	1		½ tsp	salt	½ tsp
½ tsp	caster sugar	½ tsp			freshly ground black pepper	
4 tbsp	raspberry vinegar or red wine vinegar	4 tbsp		1	cucumber, cut into 1 cm (½ inch) cubes	1

Rinse the beans under cold water, then put them into a large, heavy pan, and pour in enough cold water to cover them by about 7.5 cm (3 inches). Discard any beans that float to the surface. Cover the pan, leaving the lid ajar, and slowly bring the liquid to the boil. Boil the beans for 2 minutes, then turn off the heat, and soak the beans, covered, for at least 1 hour. (Alternatively, soak the beans overnight in cold water.)

Preheat the oven to 240°C (475°F or Mark 9).

If the beans have absorbed all of their soaking liquid, pour in enough water to cover them again by about 7.5 cm (3 inches). Bring to the boil, reduce the heat to maintain a simmer, and cook until they are tender – about 1hour.

While the beans are cooking, put the aubergine cubes into a lightly oiled baking dish and bake until they are golden-brown – about 20 minutes. Meanwhile, combine the onion with the sugar and 2 tablespoons of the vinegar; set the mixture aside. When the aubergine cubes are browned, transfer them to a bowl; toss the cubes with the remaining 2 tablespoons of vinegar and set the bowl aside until the beans finish cooking.

Drain the cooked beans and rinse them under cold running water. Combine them with the marinated aubergine and onion. Add the sage, garlic, salt, some pepper and the cucumber, and mix well. Serve the salad at room temperature or chill it for at least 30 minutes before serving.

Red and White Bean Salad

Serves 8
as a first
course or
side dish

Working
time: about
25 minutes

Total time:
about
9 Hours and
20 minutes
(includes
soaking)

Calories
200
Protein
11g
Cholesterol
0mg
Total fat
3g
Saturated fat
0g
Sodium
95mg

250 g	red kidney beans, soaked for 8 hours (or overnight) and drained	8 oz
250 g	dried haricot or cannellini beans soaked for 8 hours (or overnight) and drained	8 oz
1	small celeriac	1
1	small onion, thinly sliced	1

1	large ripe tomato, chopped	1
2 tsp	finely chopped fresh ginger root	2 tsp
4 tbsp	red wine vinegar	4 tbsp
¼ tsp	salt	¼ tsp
	freshly ground black pepper	
1 tbsp	chopped fresh coriander	1 tbsp
1½ tbsp	safflower oil	1½ tbsp

Put the kidney beans and haricot beans into two separate large saucepans with enough cold water to cover by about 7.5 cm (3 inch). Bring to the boil. Boil the kidney beans for 10 minutes, then turn down the heat to simmer. When the haricot beans come to the boil, turn the heat down to simmer. Simmer both beans until tender – 50 to 60 minutes cooking time in all.

Meanwhile, peel the celeriac and cut it into 1 cm (½ inch) cubes. Transfer the cubes to a salad bowl and toss them with the onion, ginger and vinegar. Set aside.

Drain the cooked beans and rinse them under cold water. Drain again and add them to the bowl with the salt, some pepper, the coriander, tomato and oil; mix well, and serve chilled or at room temperature.

Editor's Note: Instead of overnight soaking, the beans can be put in a pan with enough cold water to cover by 7.5 cm (3 inches), boiled for 2 minutes, then left to stand (off the heat and covered) for at least 1 hour, and drained.

Lentil and Mushroom Salad

Serves 6
as a
side dish

Working
time: about
40 minutes

Total time:
about
1 hour and
40 minutes
(includes
chilling)

Calories
165

Protein
8g

Cholesterol
0mg

Total fat
5g

Saturated fat
1g

Sodium
165mg

140 g	lentils, picked over	**4¼ oz**
1	small onion, studded with 4 whole cloves	**1**
1	bay leaf	**1**
2 tsp	fresh thyme, or ½ tsp dried thyme	**2 tsp**
3	carrots, thinly sliced	**3**
3	sticks celery, sliced	**3**
3	spring onions, trimmed and thinly sliced	**3**
175 g	mushrooms, wiped clean, trimmed and thinly sliced	**6 oz**
2 tbsp	fresh lemon juice	**2 tbsp**
3 or 4	cos lettuce leaves, chiffonade	**3 or 4**
2	ripe tomatoes, each cut into 8 wedges	**2**
1 tbsp	chopped parsley	**1 tbsp**
	Spicy Mustard Vinaigrette	
1 tbsp	Dijon mustard	**1 tbsp**
2 tbsp	fresh lemon juice	**2 tbsp**
2 tsp	Tabasco sauce	**2 tsp**
2	garlic cloves, finely chopped	**2**
¼ tsp	salt	**¼ tsp**
	freshly ground black pepper	
2 tbsp	virgin olive oil	**2 tbsp**

Rinse the lentils and put into a pan with 1 litre (1¾ pints) of water. Add the onion, bay leaf and thyme, and bring to boil. Reduce the heat to a simmer and cook until tender – about 25 minutes. Drain, discard the onion and the bay leaf, and transfer to a large bowl. Add the carrots, celery and spring onions, and toss well.

Put the mushrooms and the lemon juice into a pan; pour in water to just cover the mushrooms, and bring to boil. Cover, and simmer until

tender – about 5 minutes. Drain and add them to the bowl containing the other vegetables.

To prepare the vinaigrette, whisk together the mustard, lemon juice, Tabasco sauce, garlic, salt, some pepper and the oil. Pour over the lentils, toss well, and refrigerate for 1 hour.

To serve, mound the mixture in the centre of a plate and arrange the lettuce around the lentils. Garnish with the tomato wedges and sprinkle the chopped parsley over all.

Curried Black-Eyed Peas

Serves 6 as a side dish

Working time: about 20 minutes

Total time: about 2 hours and 30 minutes (includes soaking and chilling

Calories 105

Protein 5g

Cholesterol 0mg

Total fat 3g

Saturated fat 0g

Sodium 100mg

170 g	black-eyed peas, picked over	**6 oz**	**½ tbsp**	honey	**½ tbsp**
¼ tsp	salt	**¼ tsp**	**1¼ tsp**	curry powder	**1¼ tsp**
12.5 cl	unsalted chicken stock	**4 fl oz**		freshly ground black pepper	
2	bunches spring onions, trimmed	**2**	**1 tbsp**	virgin olive oil	**1 tbsp**
	and cut into 2.5 cm (1 inch) lengths		**½**	sweet red pepper, seeded,	**½**
1½ tbsp	fresh lemon juice	**1½ tbsp**		deribbed and cut into bâtonnets	
1 tbsp	red or white wine vinegar	**1 tbsp**			

Rinse the black-eyed peas under cold running water, then put them into a large saucepan, and pour in enough cold water to cover them by about 7.5 cm (3 inches). Discard any peas that float to the surface. Bring the water to the boil and cook the peas for 2 minutes. Turn off the heat, partially cover the pan, and soak the peas for at least 1 hour. (Alternatively, soak the peas overnight in cold water.)

Bring the peas to a simmer over medium-low heat and tightly cover the pan. Cook, occasionally skimming any foam from the surface, until they begin to soften – about 45 minutes. Stir in the salt and continue cooking until they are tender – about 15 minutes. If the peas appear to be

drying out at any point, pour in more water.

While the peas are cooking, heat the stock in a large frying pan over medium heat. Add the spring onions and partially cover the pan. Cook the spring onions, stirring often, until almost all the liquid has evaporated – 8 to 10 minutes. Transfer the contents of the pan to a bowl.

In a smaller bowl, combine the lemon juice, vinegar, honey, curry powder and some pepper. Whisk in the oil and set the dressing aside.

Transfer the cooked peas to a colander; rinse and drain them. Add the peas and the red pepper to the spring onions in the bowl. Pour the dressing over all and toss the salad well. Chill the salad for at least 30 minutes before serving.

Chick-Pea Salad with Cucumber and Dill Sauce

Serves 6 as a side dish

Working time: about 25 minutes

Total time: about 2 hours and 30 minutes (includes soaking)

200 g	chick-peas, picked over	**7 oz**
2	cucumbers	**2**
1	large tomato, skinned, seeded and coarsely chopped	**1**
4 tbsp	finely cut fresh dill	**4 tbsp**

12.5 cl	plain low-fat yogurt	**4 fl oz**
2 tbsp	soured cream	**2 tbsp**
¼ tsp	salt	**¼ tsp**
	freshly ground black pepper	

Rinse the chick-peas under cold running water, then put them in a large, heavy frying pan and pour in enough cold water to cover them by about 7.5 cm (3 inches). Discard any that float to the surface. Cover the pan, leaving the lid ajar, and slowly bring the liquid to the boil over medium-low heat. Boil the chick-peas for 2 minutes, then turn off the heat and soak them for at least 1 hour. (Alternatively, soak the peas overnight in cold water.) If they absorb all the liquid, add enough water to cover them again by about 7.5 cm (3 inches). Bring the liquid to the boil, reduce the heat to maintain a strong simmer, and cook the peas until they are tender – about 1 hour.

Drain the peas, rinse them under cold running water, and transfer them to a salad bowl.

Cut one cucumber into thin slices and set them aside. Peel the remaining cucumber and seed it. Finely chop the flesh and place it on a large square of doubled muslin. Gather the ends and twist them to wring out as much moisture as possible from the cucumber. Discard the juice.

Combine the chopped cucumber, tomato, dill, yogurt, soured cream, salt and some pepper with the chick-peas, and gently toss the mixture. Serve the salad garnished with the reserved cucumber slices.

Couscous with Mange-Tout and Wild Mushrooms

Serves 6
as a first
course or
side dish

Working
time: about
20 minutes

Total time:
about
35 minutes

Calories
135
Protein
5g
Cholesterol
0mg
Total fat
4g
Saturated fat
1g
Sodium
150mg

35 cl	unsalted chicken stock	12 fl oz	1 tsp	fresh thyme, or ¼ tsp dried thyme	1 tsp
4 tbsp	chopped shallot	4 tbsp	125 g	.mange-tout, stems and strings removed, each cut diagonally into 3 pieces	4 oz
2½ tbsp	fresh lemon juice	2½ tbsp			
175 g	couscous	6 oz			
6 tbsp	coarsely chopped fresh coriander	6 tbsp	¼ tsp	salt	¼ tsp
			1 tsp	red wine vinegar	1 tsp
1½ tbsp	virgin olive oil	1½ tbsp	1	oakleaf or red-leaf lettuce, washed and dried	1
125 g	fresh ceps, chanterelles or other wild mushrooms, wiped clean and sliced	4 oz		freshly ground black pepper	

Pour the stock into a large pan; add 2 tablespoons of the shallot, 2 tablespoons of the lemon juice and some pepper. Bring to the boil, then stir in the couscous and half of the coriander. Cover the pan tightly and remove it from the heat; let it stand while you complete the salad.

Meanwhile, heat 1 tablespoon of the oil in a large, heavy frying pan over medium-high heat. When the oil is hot, add the mushrooms, thyme and the remaining shallot. Sauté the mushrooms until they begin to brown – about 4 minutes. Stir in the mange-tout, the salt and some pepper. Cook the mixture, stirring frequently, for

2 minutes more. Remove from heat.

Transfer the couscous to a large bowl and fluff it with a fork. In a small bowl, combine the vinegar, the remaining oil, the remaining lemon juice and the remaining coriander. Dribble this vinaigrette over the couscous and fluff it once again to distribute the dressing evenly. Add the contents of the frying pan to the bowl, using a rubber spatula to scrape out the flavour-rich juices. Toss the salad well and chill it for at least 15 minutes.

To serve, arrange the lettuce on a platter and mound the salad on top of the leaves.

Pasta with Prawns, Aubergine and Yellow Squash

Serves 6
as a
main course

Working
time: about
35 minutes

Total time:
about
45 minutes

Calories
260
Protein
16g
Cholesterol
80mg
Total fat
6g
Saturated fat
1g
Sodium
250mg

2 tbsp	virgin olive oil	2 tbsp
2½ tbsp	fresh lime juice	2½ tbsp
1	aubergine halved lengthwise, halves cut crosswise into 1 cm (½ inch) slices	1
250 g	spinach pasta spirals or other fancy spinach pasta	8 oz
1	large yellow squash or courgette, halved lengthwise, halves cut diagonally into 1 cm (½ inch) slices	1

250 g	ripe tomatoes	8 oz
2	shallots, finely chopped	2
350 g	fresh prawns, peeled	12 oz
1 tsp	fresh thyme, or ¼ tsp dried thyme	1 tsp
¼ tsp	salt	¼ tsp
	freshly ground black pepper	
60 g	goat cheese	2 oz
4 tbsp	plain low-fat yogurt	4 tbsp
2 tbsp	milk	2 tbsp

Preheat the grill. Bring 3 litres (5 pints) of water to the boil in a large saucepan.

Mix 1 tbsp of the oil with 1 tbsp of the lime juice and brush both sides of the aubergine. Set slices on a baking sheet and grill on both sides until lightly browned – 3 to 4 minutes. Cool before transferring to a bowl. Refrigerate.

Add the pasta to the water with 1½ tsps of salt. Start testing the pasta after 10 mins and cook until al dente. Drain, rinse, and drain again. Add the pasta to the bowl with the aubergine.

While cooking, place tomatoes stem end down. Cut the flesh in wide, flat sections; discard the core and seeds. Slice into strips

5 mm (¼ inch) wide and set them aside.

Heat the remaining oil in a frying pan over medium-high heat. When hot, add the squash and shallots. Cook, stirring, for 1 min. Add the prawns, thyme, salt, some pepper and remaining lime juice; sauté until the prawns are just cooked – 2 mins. Stir in the tomato and cook for 30 secs. Transfer from pan to the bowl with the pasta and aubergine, toss well; refrigerate.

To prepare the dressing, put the cheese, yogurt, milk and a liberal grinding of black pepper into a blender/processor. Purée, scraping the sides at least once. Dress the salad; toss well and chill briefly before serving.

Asian Pasta and Garter Bean Salad

Serves 8
as a
side dish

Working
(and total)
time: about
30 minutes

Calories
150

Protein
5g

Cholesterol
0mg

Total fat
3g

Saturated fat
0g

Sodium
20mg

250 g	dried Asian wheat noodles (somen) or dried vermicelli	8 oz		**Celery-Sesame Dressing**		
250 g	garter beans or French beans, trimmed and cut into 6 cm (2½ inch) lengths	8 oz	60 g	celery, chopped	2 oz
			45 g	onion, chopped	1½oz
3	spring onions, trimmed, finely chopped	3	2 tbsp	rice vinegar	2 tbsp
			1 tbsp	safflower oil	1 tbsp
1 tbsp	finely chopped fresh coriander	1 tbsp	1 tbsp	low-sodium soy sauce or shoyu	1 tbsp
1 tbsp	roasted, unsalted peanuts, chopped	1 tbsp	1 tbsp	finely chopped fresh ginger root	1 tbsp
			1 tsp	dark sesame oil	1 tsp
			1	clove garlic, finely chopped	1
			2 tbsp	fresh lemon juice	2 tbsp
			¼ tsp	chili paste	¼ tsp

Bring 4 litres (7 pints) of water to the boil in a large pan. Add the pasta and cook it until it is *al dente* – 3 to 5 minutes. Drain the pasta and rinse it under cold water. Transfer it to a large bowl of cold water and set aside.

Bring 2 litres (3½ pints) of water to the boil in a large saucepan. Add the beans and blanch them until just tender – about 3 minutes. Drain and refresh the beans under cold running water. Drain and set aside.

To make the dressing, put the celery, onion,

vinegar, safflower oil, soy sauce, ginger, sesame oil, garlic, lemon juice and chili paste into a blender or food processor. Purée the dressing until it is smooth.

Drain the pasta well and transfer it to a bowl. Pour in the dressing, spring onions and coriander and toss. Heap the dressed noodles or vermicelli in the centre of a platter or serving dish, then poke the beans one at a time into the mound to form a sunburst pattern. Sprinkle on the peanuts. Serve the salad at once.

Wagon-Wheel Pasta Salad

Serves 12
as a
first course

Working
and total
time: about
35 minutes

Calories
210
Protein
7g
Cholesterol
0mg
Total fat
4g
Saturated fat
1g
Sodium
170mg

8	sun-dried tomatoes	8	4 tbsp	red wine vinegar	4 tbsp
500 g	wagon wheels or other fancy pasta	1 lb	¼ tsp	salt	¼ tsp
300 g	fresh shelled broad beans, skinned, or frozen broad beans thawed	10 oz	2 tbsp	freshly ground black pepper cut chives	2 tbsp
2	garlic cloves, peeled	2	1 tbsp	virgin olive oil	1 tbsp
			4	cherry tomatoes, cut into quarters	4

Put the sun-dried tomatoes into a small heatproof bowl and pour 12.5 cl (4 fl oz) of boiling water over them. Let the tomatoes soak for 20 minutes.

While the tomatoes are soaking, add the pasta to 4 litres (7 pints) of boiling water with 1 teaspoon of salt. Begin testing for readiness after 5 minutes and cook it until it is *al dente*. Drain the pasta and rinse; drain it once more and transfer the pasta to a large bowl. Add the fresh broad beans to 1 litre (1¾ pints) of boiling water

and cook them until barely tender – 8 to 10 minutes. Drain the beans and set them aside. (If you are using frozen beans, cook them in 4 tablespoons of boiling water for 5 minutes.)

In a blender or food processor, purée the sun-dried tomatoes along with their soaking liquid, the garlic, vinegar, salt and some pepper. Add the broad beans, chives, cherry tomatoes, oil and tomato-garlic purée to the pasta; toss well and serve the salad immediately

Pasta Salad with Black Bean Sauce

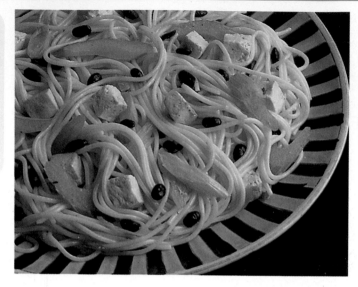

Serves 8
as a
main course
at lunch

Working
time: about
15 minutes

Totat time:
about
1 hour and
30 minutes
(includes
chilling)

Calories
290

Protein
12g

Cholesterol
0mg

Total fat
7g

Saturated fat
1g

Sodium
495mg

500 g	vermicelli (or other thin pasta)	1 lb
2 tbsp	peanut oil	2 tbsp
2	small dried hot red chili peppers, coarsely chopped	2
3	spring onions, trimmed and sliced diagonally	3
2	garlic cloves, finely chopped	2

30 g	fermented black beans, rinsed	1 oz
250 g	firm tofu, cut into 2 cm (¾ inch) cubes	8 oz
12.5 cl	unsalted chicken stock	4 fl oz
2	celery sticks, sliced diagonally	2
¼ tsp	salt	¼ tsp
4 tsp	rice vinegar	4 tsp

Add the vermicelli with 1 teaspoon of salt to 4 litres (7 pints) of boiling water. Start testing the pasta after 5 minutes and cook it until it is *al dente*. Drain the pasta, transfer it to a large bowl of cold water, and set it aside while you make the sauce.

To begin the sauce, heat the peanut oil and chili peppers in a small saucepan; when the oil begins to smoke, remove the pan from the heat and set it aside to cool for 5 minutes. Strain the oil into a heavy frying pan. Discard the chili peppers.

Put the spring onions and garlic into the pan containing the peanut oil; cook them over medium heat for 2 minutes. Add the black beans, tofu and stock, and simmer the mixture for 5 minutes. Stir in the celery and salt, and continue cooking the mixture until the celery is barely tender – about 2 minutes more.

While the sauce is simmering, drain the noodles well. Transfer them to a large bowl and toss with vinegar. Pour the hot sauce over all and mix thoroughly. Refrigerate the salad for at least 1 hour before serving.

Buckwheat Noodle Salad

Serves 8 as a first course

Working (and total) time: about 25 minutes

Calories 130
Protein 3g
Cholesterol 0mg
Total fat 3g
Saturated fat 0g
Sodium 135mg

250 g	dried buckwheat noodles (soba)	**8 oz**
1	sweet red pepper, seeded, deribbed and julienned	**1**
3	Chinese cabbage leaves, torn in small pieces	**3**

Ginger-Lime Dressing

1	small shallot, finely chopped	**1**
2.5 cm	piece fresh ginger root, peeled and coarsely chopped	**1 inch**
1	lime, rind grated and juice reserved	**1**
¼ tsp	salt	**¼ tsp**
½ tsp	honey	**½ tsp**
1½ tbsp	safflower oil	**1½ tbsp**
½ tsp	dark sesame oil	**½ tsp**

Add the noodles to 2 litres (3½ pints) of boiling water in a large saucepan. Start testing them for readiness after 5 minutes and cook them until they are *al dente*. Drain the noodles and rinse them well; then cover them with cold water and set them aside.

To make the dressing, place the ginger, lime rind and salt in a mortar; mash them with a pestle until the ginger is reduced to very small pieces. Stir in the lime juice, honey, shallot and two oils. Drain the noodles and transfer them to a serving platter. Pour the dressing over them and toss with the pepper strips. Serve immediately, surrounded by the cabbage.

Ditalini Salad with Smoked Salmon

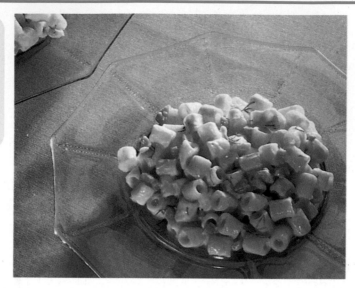

Serves 8 as a first course or side dish

Working time: about 20 minutes

Total time: about 30 minutes

Calories 130

Protein 5g

Cholesterol 3mg

Total fat 1g

Saturated fat 0g

Sodium 110mg

250 g	ditalini or elbow macaroni	**8 oz**
12.5 cl	plain low-fat yogurt	**4 fl oz**
1 tbsp	brown sugar	**1 tbsp**
¾ tsp	dry mustard	**¾ tsp**
2 tbsp	cut fresh dill	**2 tbsp**
2 tbsp	fresh lemon juice	**2 tbsp**
¼ tsp	salt	**¼ tsp**
	freshly ground black pepper	
30 g	smoked salmon, cut into 5 mm (¼ inch) cubes	**1 oz**

Add the pasta to 4 litres (7 pints) of boiling water with 1½ teaspoons of salt. Begin testing the pasta after 5 minutes and cook it until it is *al dente*. Drain the pasta and rinse it under cold running water; drain it once more and transfer it to a large bowl.

To prepare the dressing, whisk together the yogurt, brown sugar, mustard, dill, lemon juice, salt and some pepper in a small bowl.

Add the salmon to the pasta, pour the dressing over all, and toss well; serve the salad immediately.

Editor's Note: Both the dressing and pasta may be prepared 1 hour before serving time; they should be refrigerated separately and assembled at the last possible moment.

Monkfish Salad with Green and White Linguine

Serves 4 as a main course

Working time: about 50 minutes

Total time: about 1 hour and 15 minutes

Calories 440

Protein 30g

Cholesterol 45mg

Total fat 10g

Saturated fat 1g

Sodium 290mg

500 g	monkfish fillets, rinsed, patted dry and cut into 5 cm (2 inch) pieces	**1 lb**
1	lemon, juice only	**1**
1 tbsp	chopped fresh tyme, or 1 tsp dried thyme	**1 tbsp**
⅛ tsp	cayenne pepper	**⅛ tsp**
¼ tsp	salt	**¼ tsp**
	freshly ground black pepper	
2	leeks, trimmed, split, washed, and julienned	**2**
1	carrot, julienned	**1**

1	stick celery, julienned	**1**
125 g	spinach linguine or narrow fettuccine	**4 oz**
	Dill Dressing	
½ tsp	Dijon mustard	**½ tsp**
1 tbsp	finely cut fresh dill, or 2 tsp dried dill	**1 tbsp**
	freshly ground black pepper	
1 tbsp	fresh lemon juice	**1 tbsp**
2 tbsp	safflower oil	**2 tbsp**

Place the fish in a shallow dish. In a small bowl, combine the lemon juice with the thyme, cayenne pepper, salt and black pepper. Pour over the fish and marinate for at least 30 minutes.

Toss the leek, carrot and celery in a bowl with a grinding of black pepper; set aside.

To prepare the dressing, combine the mustard, dill, some pepper and the lemon juice in a bowl. Pour in the oil steadily; whisking until the dressing is combined, then set aside.

Add the linguine with ½ tsp of salt to 4 litres (7 pints) of boiling water. Test the pasta after

8 mins and cook until *al dente*. Drain and rinse, transfer to a bowl and toss with half of the dressing; set aside.

Pour water into a shallow pan – 2.5 cm (1 inch) deep. Put the vegetables in a steamer and bring to the boil, tightly cover, and steam for 1 min. Place the fish on the vegetables, cover again and steam until it is opaque and feels firm – 1 to 2 mins. Remove the steamer and let cool.

Mound the linguine on a platter. Top the pasta with the fish and vegetables. Pour the remaining dressing over the salad and serve.

Trout Salad with Basil Vinaigrette

Serves 4 as a first course

Working time: about 20 minutes

Total time: about 40 minutes

Calories 200
Protein 22g
Cholesterol 65mg
Total fat 10g
Saturated fat 1g
Sodium 185mg

2	trout (500 g/1 lb each), filleted	2
2 tbsp	sherry vinegar	2 tbsp
1 tbsp	finely chopped shallot	1 tbsp
1	small garlic clove, finely chopped	1
¼ tsp	salt	¼ tsp
⅛ tsp	white pepper	⅛ tsp
1 tbsp	safflower oil	1 tbsp
4 tbsp	loosely packed fresh basil leaves, cut into chiffonade	4 tbsp
2	ripe tomatoes, each cut into 6 slices	2
4	sprigs fresh basil	4

Lay a trout fillet on a cutting board with its skinned side down. With a small knife, cut along one side of the line of bones running the length of the fillet. Make a similar cut along the other side of the line of bones; discard the thin strip of flesh and bones thus formed. You should now have two pieces, one twice the width of the other. Halve the larger piece lengthwise. Fold each piece into a loose 'bow' and set the bow on a heatproof plate. Repeat these steps to fashion the remaining fillets into bows.

Pour enough water into a large pan to fill it about 2.5 cm (1 inch) deep. Place two or three small bowls of equal height in the bottom of the pan; set the plate on top of the bowls. Cover the

pan, bring to the boil, and steam the fish until it is opaque and firm to the touch – about 2 minutes. Remove the plate and set it aside while you prepare the dressing.

Whisk together the vinegar, shallot, garlic, salt, pepper, oil and half of the basil. Pour this dressing over the fish bows and refrigerate them until they are cool – about 20 minutes.

Arrange three tomato slices on each of four plates. Use a spatula to transfer a bow on to each tomato slice. Sprinkle the salads with the remaining chiffonade of basil. Dribble the chilled dressing over all, garnish with the basil sprigs, and serve at once.

Lobster Salad with Sweet Peppers and Coriander

Serves 4
as a main
course
or 8 as a
first course

Working
time: about
30 minutes

Total time:
about
2 hours and
30 minutes
(includes
chilling and
marinating)

Calories
190

Protein
18g

Cholesterol
65mg

Total fat
8g

Saturated fat
1g

Sodium
250mg

2	carrots, sliced into thin rounds	2
1	onion, thinly sliced	1
6 tbsp	coarsely chopped parsley	6 tbsp
2	bay leaves	2
8	black peppercorns	8
1 tbsp	vinegar, wine or lemon juice	1 tbsp
3	live lobsters (about 600 g/1¼ lb)	3
2 tbsp	fresh lemon juice	2 tbsp
2 tbsp	fresh lime juice	2 tbsp
2 tbsp	virgin olive oil	2 tbsp

1	each sweet red and yellow pepper, seeded, deribbed and cut into 5 mm (¼ inch) dice	1
½	cucumber, seeded and cut into bâtonnets	½
½	small red onion, chopped	½
1½ tbsp	chopped fresh coriander freshly ground black pepper	1½ tbsp
4 or 8	large red-leaf lettuce leaves	4 or 8
8 or 16	thin lemon wedges	8 or 16

Pour enough water into a large pot to fill it about 2.5 cm (1 inch) deep. Add the carrots, onion, parsley, bay leaves, peppercorns and vinegar, wine or lemon juice. Bring to the boil, then reduce the heat and simmer for 20 minutes. Return the liquid to the boil, add the lobsters, and cover the pot; cook the lobsters until they turn a bright red-orange – about 15 minutes. Remove the lobsters and let them cool. When the lobsters are cool enough to handle, remove the claw and tail meat and cut the tail meat into 2 cm (¾ inch) slices.

Combine the lemon and lime juices in a large bowl, then whisk in the oil. Add the lobster meat, peppers, cucumber, red onion, coriander and some pepper. Toss the mixture well, then cover the bowl. Refrigerate the salad for at least 2 hours to meld the flavours, stirring several times to distribute the dressing.

To serve, place a lettuce leaf on each plate; divide the lobster salad among the plates, then garnish each salad with two lemon wedges.

Thai Lemon-Lime Prawn Salad

Serves 4
as a main
course
at lunch

Working
(and total)
time: about
45 minutes

Calories
125
Protein
18g
Cholesterol
130mg
Total fat
1g
Saturated fat
0g
Sodium
230mg

1	tart green apple, preferably Granny Smith, peeled, cored and julienned	1
3 tbsp	fresh lemon juice	3 tbsp
3 tbsp	fresh lime juice	3 tbsp
2	shallots, thinly sliced	2
1½ tbsp	chopped fresh coriander	1½ tbsp
1 tbsp	chopped fresh mint, or 1 tsp dried mint	1 tbsp
2 tsp	fish sauce, or low-sodium soy sauce	2 tsp

2	garlic cloves, finely chopped	2
1	small dried red chili pepper, soaked in hot water for 20 minutes, drained, seeded and chopped	1
2	spring onions, thinly sliced	2
500 g	large, freshly cooked prawns, deveined if necessary and halved	1 lb
2	large round lettuces, washed and dried	2
4	mint sprigs	4

Put the julienned apple into a large bowl and toss the pieces with the lemon and lime juices, shallots, coriander, mint, fish sauce or soy sauce, garlic, chili pepper and spring onions.

Add the prawns to the bowl. Gently mix them

into the salad. Cover the bowl and refrigerate the salad for at least 30 minutes.

Serve the salad on lettuce leaves on individual plates, each portion garnished with a sprig of mint.

Prawn Salad on Fresh Pineapple-Mango Relish

Serves 8
as an main
course
at lunch

Working
time: about
30 minutes

Total time:
about
1 hour

Calories
160
Protein
13g
Cholesterol
105mg
Total fat
4g
Saturated fat
1g
Sodium
200mg

2	large ripe mangoes	2
1	pineapple, peeled and cut into 5 mm (¼ inch) cubes	1
4 tbsp	fresh lime juice	4 tbsp
30 g	fresh coriander, finely chopped	1 oz
2	sweet red peppers, halved, seeded and deribbed	2
750 g	cooked prawns, peeled, and deveined if necessary	1½ lb

4 tbsp	mayonnaise	4 tbsp
4	spring onions, trimmed and thinly sliced	4
2 tbsp	very finely chopped fresh ginger root	2 tbsp
½ tsp	salt	½ tsp
1	fresh coriander sprig for garnish	1

To prepare the relish, first peel the mangoes and remove the flesh in pieces. Purée one quarter of the flesh in a food processor or a blender, then pass it through a sieve set over a bowl. Refrigerate the purée. Cut the remaining mango pieces into 5 mm (¼ inch) cubes and place them in a bowl. Add the pineapple, lime juice and chopped coriander; stir the relish and refrigerate it.

Dice one of them pepper halves and put in a bowl with the prawns. Julienne the remaining pepper halves and set the julienne aside. Stir the

mayonnaise, mango purée, spring onions, ginger and salt into the prawn-and-pepper mixture. Chill the salad in the refrigerator for at least 30 minutes.

To serve, spoon some of the pineapple-mango relish on to a large platter and surround it with some of the prawn salad. Top the relish with the remaining prawn salad; garnish the dish with the pepper julienne and coriander sprig.

Crab Meat Salad with Grapes and Celeriac

<table>
<tr><td>Serves 4
as a main
course

Working
time: about
1 hour

Total time:
about
1 hour and
30 minutes</td></tr>
</table>

Calories
220

Protein
17g

Cholesterol
75mg

Total fat
8g

Saturated fat
1g

Sodium
225mg

350 g	white crab meat, picked over	12 oz
80 g	seedless green grapes, halved	2½ oz
80 g	seedless red grapes, halved	2½ oz
1	bunch spring onions, white parts only, julienned	1
2	large oranges, juice only of 1	2
¼ tsp	ground coriander	¼ tsp
¼ tsp	ground cumin	¼ tsp
¼ tsp	ground mace	¼ tsp
¼ tsp	ground ginger	¼ tsp
⅛ tsp	turmeric	⅛ tsp
⅛ tsp	white pepper	⅛ tsp
4 tbsp	mayonnaise	4 tbsp
250 g	celeriac, peeled and julienned	8 oz
1	lemon, juice only	1
1	lime, juice only	1
	freshly ground black pepper	
6	kumquats (optional), sliced and seeded	6

In a large bowl, combine the crab meat, green and red grapes, spring onions and orange juice. In a small bowl, blend the coriander, cumin, mace, ginger, tumeric and white pepper into the mayonnaise; add this dressing to the crab meat salad and toss the ingredients well. Refrigerate the salad for at least 30 minutes.

Put the celeriac into a third bowl; sprinkle with the lemon juice, lime juice and a generous grinding of black pepper. Toss well and chill for the same length of time as the salad.

Just before serving, segment the whole orange, cut away the peel, white pith and outer membrane, then separate from the inner membranes by slicing down to the core with a sharp knife on either side of each segment.

Mound the crab salad and the celeriac side by side on a serving platter. Garnish the salad with the orange slices and the kumquats if you are using them, and serve immediately.

Squid Salad with Spring Onions and Coriander

Serves 4
as a main
course

Working
time: about
25 minutes

Total time:
about
1 hour

Calories
175
Protein
16g
Cholesterol
223mg
Total fat
8g
Saturated fat
1g
Sodium
400mg

600 g	small squid, cleaned and skinned, tentacles reserved	1¼ lb
2 tbsp	virgin olive oil	2 tbsp
¼ tsp	salt	¼ tsp
	freshly ground black pepper	
1 tsp	coriander seeds, crushed	1 tsp
2 tbsp	sherry vinegar	2 tbsp
1 tbsp	fresh lemon juice	1 tbsp
½	sweet red pepper, seeded, deribbed and diced	½
½	sweet yellow pepper, seeded, deribbed and diced	½
4	spring onions, trimmed and sliced diagonally into thin ovals	4
1	large round lettuce, washed and dried	1
	lemon slices for garnish	1

Slice the squid pouches into thin rings. Heat 1 tablespoon of the olive oil in a large, heavy frying pan over high heat. When the oil is hot, add the squid rings and tentacles, ¼ teaspoon of the salt and some pepper. Sauté the squid, stirring constantly, until it turns opaque – about 2 minutes. Drain the squid well, reserving the cooking juices, and transfer the squid pieces to a large bowl; put the bowl in the refrigerator.

Pour the cooking juices into a small saucepan; add the crushed coriander and boil the liquid until only 2 tablespoons remain – about 3 minutes. Remove from the heat, then whisk in the vinegar, lemon juice, remaining salt and remaining oil. Pour this dressing over the squid; add the peppers and spring onions, and toss. Chill the salad for at least 30 minutes.

Just before serving the salad, grind in a generous amount of black pepper and toss well. Present the salad on the lettuce leaves, garnished with lemon slices.

Mussel Salad

Serves 4
as a
first course

Working
time: about
30 minutes

Total time:
about
1 hour

Calories
175

Protein
7g

Cholesterol
25mg

Total fat
5g

Saturated fat
1g

Sodium
125mg

90 g	rice	3 oz
1 tbsp	fennel seeds	1 tbsp
2 tbsp	finely chopped sweet green pepper	2 tbsp
4 tbsp	finely chopped red onion	4 tbsp
1	small ripe tomato, skinned, seeded and chopped	1

1	small garlic clove, finely chopped	1
1 tbsp	grated horseradish, drained	1 tbsp
3 tbsp	white wine vinegar	3 tbsp
24	mussels, scrubbed and debearded	24
1 tbsp	virgin olive oil	1 tbsp
	parsley sprigs for garnish	

Put the rice, the fennel seeds and ¼ litre (8 fl oz) of water into a small saucepan over medium-high heat. Bring to the boil, then reduce the heat, cover the pan, and simmer the rice until it is tender – 20 to 25 minutes. Set the rice aside.

While the rice simmers, prepare the marinade. Mix together the green pepper, onion, tomato, garlic, horseradish and vinegar in a bowl. Set the marinade aside while you cook the mussels.

Bring ¼ litre (8 fl oz) of water to the boil in a large pan. Add the mussels and cover the pan. Steam the mussels until they open – 2 to 3 minutes. Discard any that remain closed. Strain the liquid through a sieve lined with double muslin, taking care not to pour any sand into the sieve. Reserve the liquid.

Using a slotted spoon, transfer the mussels to a large bowl. When the mussels are cool enough to handle, remove them from their shells, reserving one half of each shell. Dip each mussel into the reserved liquid to rinse away any residual sand. Pat the mussels dry, then add them to the marinade, and let them stand at room temperature for 30 minutes.

Stir the rice and oil into the marinated mussels. Fill each reserved mussel shell with one mussel and about 2 teaspoons of the rice-and-vegetable mixture. Arrange the stuffed shells on a platter; garnish the platter with the parsley just before serving.

Turkey Salad with Green and Red Grapes

Serves 4
as a
main course

Working
time: about
20 minutes

Total time:
about
1 hour and
30 minutes

Calories
290

Protein
27g

Cholesterol
60mg

Total fat
17g

Saturated fat
2g

Sodium
200mg

500 g	skinless turkey breast meat	1 lb	80 g	seedless green grapes	2½ oz
2 tbsp	fresh lemon juice	2 tbsp	80 g	seedless red grapes	2½ oz
1 tbsp	virgin olive oil	1 tbsp	3	spring onions, trimmed and thinly sliced	3
1 tbsp	fresh thyme, 1 tsp dried thyme	1 tbsp	4 tbsp	vinaigrette	4 tbsp
⅛ tsp	salt	⅛ tsp	1	small red-leaf lettuce, washed and dried	1
	freshly ground black pepper				
2 tbsp	sliced almonds	2 tbsp			

Preheat the oven to 190°C (375°F or Mark 5). Put the turkey meat in a small baking dish and sprinkle it with the lemon juice, oil, thyme, salt and some pepper. Rub the seasonings into the meat and let it marinate at room temperature for 20 minutes.

At the end of the marinating time, roast the meat, turning it once, until it feels firm but springy to the touch – about 20 minutes.

While the meat is cooking, spread the almonds on a small baking sheet and toast them in the oven until they are golden-brown – about 4 minutes. Set the toasted almonds aside.

When the turkey has finished cooking, remove it from the oven and let it cool in the dish. As soon as the meat is cool enough to handle, remove it from the dish and cut it diagonally into thin slices. Lay the slices in the pan juices and refrigerate them for at least 30 minutes.

To assemble the salad, combine the grapes, spring onions and vinaigrette in a bowl. Arrange the turkey slices on the lettuce leaves and mound the grapes and spring onions on top; sprinkle the salad with the toasted almonds and serve immediately.

Chicken and Avocado Salad with Ricotta and Chives

Serves 4
as a
main course

Working
time: about
20 minutes

Total time:
about
50 minutes

Calories
315

Protein
40g

Cholesterol
100mg

Total fat
17g

Saturated fat
4g

Sodium
265mg

1 tsp	safflower oil	1 tsp
4	chicken breasts, skinned and boned (500 g/1 lb)	4
¼ tsp	salt	¼ tsp
	freshly ground black pepper	
250 g	low-fat ricotta cheese	8 oz
1 tbsp	low-fat plain yogurt	1 tbsp
2 tbsp	chopped chives	2 tbsp
1	spring onion, very finely sliced	1

1	head of radicchio or red-leaf lettuce, washed and dried	1
1	ripe avocado, stone removed, peeled, flesh rubbed with 1 tbsp fresh lemon juice	1
1	tomato, seeded and finely chopped (optional)	1
6	fresh basil leaves, thinly sliced (optional)	6

Heat the safflower oil in a large, heavy frying pan over very low heat. Season the chicken breasts and place them in a pan. Set a heavy plate on top of the chicken breasts to weight them down so that they will cook evenly. Cook the breasts on one side for 5 minutes; turn them over, again cover them with the plate, and cook them for 3 to 4 minutes more. The meat should feel firm but springy to the touch, with no traces of pink along the edges. Transfer the chicken to a plate and refrigerate while you prepare the rest of the salad.

Put the ricotta, yogurt, chives and spring onion into a bowl. Mix them well together, then cover the bowl and leave it to stand in a cool place for about 30 minutes.

Arrange a few radicchio or lettuce leaves on four plates. Slice the cooked chicken breasts diagonally and fan out each one of the leaves. Cut the peeled avocado into thin slices and tuck these between the chicken slices, then spoon a neat mound of the ricotta mixture on to the base of each chicken fan. If using, sprinkle the chopped tomato and basil over the top and, if you like, a little freshly ground pepper.

Curried Chicken Salad with Raisins

Serves 6 as a main course

Working time: about 20 minutes

Total time: about 1 hour

Cal.
25

Protein
20g

Cholesterol
55mg

Total fat
9g

Saturated fat
2g

Sodium
190mg

1 tsp	safflower oil	1 tsp
6	chicken breasts, skinned and boned (about 750 g/1½ lb)	6
¼ tsp	salt	¼ tsp
75 g	raisins	2½ oz
1	large carrot, grated	1
1	onion, grated	1
1	stick celery, chopped	1
3 tbsp	fresh lemon juice	3 tbsp
1 tbsp	curry powder	1 tbsp
1 tbsp	honey	1 tbsp
4 tbsp	mayonnaise	4 tbsp
100 g	radishes, julienned	3½ oz
½ tbsp	virgin olive oil	½ tbsp
1	small cos lettuce, washed and dried	1
2	ripe tomatoes, cut into wedges	2

Heat the safflower oil in a large, heavy frying pan over low heat. Sprinkle the chicken breasts with the salt and place them in the pan. Set a heavy plate on top of the chicken breasts to weight them down so that they will cook evenly. Cook the breasts on the first side for 5 minutes; turn them over, weight them down again, and cook them on the second side for 3 to 4 minutes. The meat should feel firm but springy to the touch, with no traces of pink along the edges. Transfer the breasts to a plate and allow them to cool. When the chicken is cool, cut it into 2.5 cm (1 inch) cubes.

In a large mixing bowl, toss the chicken cubes with the raisins, grated carrot and onion, chopped celery, lemon juice, curry powder, honey and mayonnaise. Chill the salad for at least 30 minutes.

Toss the radish julienne with the olive oil in a small bowl. Mound the chicken salad on the lettuce leaves, and garnish each plate with the radish julienne and the tomato wedges. Serve immediately.

Lamb Salad with Fig Sauce

Serves 8
as a
first course

Working
time: about
35 minutes

Total time:
about
2 hours

Calories
385
Protein
24g
Cholesterol
60mg
Total fat
22g
Saturated fat
10g
Sodium
155mg

1 tbsp	safflower oil	**1 tbsp**
1.5 kg	leg of lamb shank end, trimmed of fat	**3 lb**
¼ tsp	salt	**¼ tsp**
	freshly ground black pepper	
2 tbsp	virgin olive oil	**2 tbsp**
175 g	dried figs, quartered	**6 oz**
4 tbsp	chopped shallot	**4 tbsp**

½ tbsp	fresh thyme, or ½ tsp dried thyme	**½ tbsp**
¼ litre	unsalted veal or chicken stock	**8 fl oz**
5 tbsp	sherry vinegar or red wine vinegar	**5 tbsp**
1	large Batavian endive, washed and dried several thyme sprigs for garnish	**1**

Preheat the oven to 180°C (350°F or Mark 4). Heat the safflower oil in a large shallow flameproof casserole over medium-high heat. Add the lamb and brown it well – 10 to 12 minutes. Season, then transfer to the oven. For medium rare meat, roast the lamb for about 1 hour; for medium, roast the lamb for 1¼ hours. Remove from the casserole and set it aside to cool.

Return the casserole to the stove, over medium heat. Add 1 tbsp of the olive oil, figs, shallot, thyme and some pepper. Cook, stirring frequently, for 3 minutes. Pour in the stock and 4 tbsp of the vinegar. Reduce the heat and simmer, stirring occasionally, for 5 minutes.

Remove 16 fig quarters from the casserole and set them aside. To make the sauce, purée the remaining contents of the casserole in a processor/blender. Scrape down the sides at least once during the process. Transfer the sauce to a bowl and chill it.

When the lamb has cooled, slice it thinly against the grain. Toss the Batavian endive with the remaining olive oil, the remaining vinegar and a generous grinding of black pepper.

Spread the endive on individual salad plates and arrange the lamb slices on top. Pour the fig sauce over the lamb; garnish with the reserved fig quarters and thyme sprigs. Serve immediately.

Pot-au-Feu Salad

Serves 4
as a
main course

Working
time: about
50 minutes

Total time:
about
5 hours and
30 minutes
(includes
chilling)

Calories
510
Protein
33g
Cholesterol
100mg
Total fat
23g
Saturated fat
5g
Sodium
400mg

½ tbsp	safflower oil	½ tbsp	2	turnips, peeled, each cut into wedges	2
500 g	beef topside, trimmed of fat	1 lb	4	leeks, trimmed, split lengthwise and washed thoroughly to remove all grit	4
1	calf's foot or 2 pig's trotters	1			
¼ tsp	salt	¼ tsp	4	small round red potatoes, each cut into wedges	4
2 litres	unsalted veal or chicken stock	3½ pints			
			2 tbsp	chopped parsley	2 tbsp
4	carrots, cut into 5 cm (2 inch) segments, each segment quartered lengthwise	4	1	lettuce, washed and dried	1
			12.5 cl	mayonnaise	4 fl oz

Heat the safflower oil in a large pan over medium-high heat. Add the beef and brown it – about 10 minutes. Add the calf's foot or pig's trotters, the salt and the stock; bring to a simmer and cook it for 1½ hours. Strain and reserve the broth. Reserve the beef; discard the other solids.

Rinse the pan and return the beef and broth to it. Add the carrots, turnips, leeks and potatoes, and bring to the boil. Reduce the heat and simmer until tender – about 35 minutes. Remove the pan from the heat and cool to room temperature – about 30 minutes. Spoon the fat from the surface, then blot any remaining traces

with a paper towel. Remove the beef and vegetables from the broth and refrigerate. Pour ½ litre (16 fl oz) of the broth into a bowl and stir the parsley into it, then divide the broth amoung four ramekins; chill these until the broth has set – about 2 hours.

Slice the beef and arrange it with the vegetables on individual lettuce-lined plates. Briefly dip the bottom of a ramekin into hot water; invert on to one of the plates to release the jellied broth, then lift away the mould. Unmould the others in the same way. Serve the salads with the mayonnaise alongside.

Useful weights and measures

Weight Equivalents

Avoirdupois		Metric
1 ounce	=	28.35 grams
1 pound	=	254.6 grams
2.3 pounds	=	1 kilogram

Liquid Measurements

$^1/_4$ pint	=	$1^1/_2$ decilitres
$^1/_2$ pint	=	$^1/_4$ litre
scant 1 pint	=	$^1/_2$ litre
$1^3/_4$ pints	=	1 litre
1 gallon	=	4.5 litres

Liquid Measures

1 pint	=	20 fl oz	=	32 tablespoons
$^1/_2$ pint	=	10 fl oz	=	16 tablespoons
$^1/_4$ pint	=	5 fl oz	=	8 tablespoons
$^1/_8$ pint	=	$2^1/_2$ fl oz	=	4 tablespoons
$^1/_{16}$ pint	=	$1^1/_4$ fl oz	=	2 tablespoons

Solid Measures

1 oz almonds, ground = $3^3/_4$ level tablespoons
1 oz breadcrumbs fresh = 7 level tablespoons
1 oz butter, lard = 2 level tablespoons
1 oz cheese, grated = $3^1/_2$ level tablespoons
1 oz cocoa = $2^3/_4$ level tablespoons
1 oz desiccated coconut = $4^1/_2$ tablespoons
1 oz cornflour = $2^1/_2$ tablespoons
1 oz custard powder = $2^1/_2$ tablespoons
1 oz curry powder and spices = 5 tablespoons
1 oz flour = 2 level tablespoons
1 oz rice, uncooked = $1^1/_2$ tablespoons
1 oz sugar, caster and granulated = 2 tablespoons
1 oz icing sugar = $2^1/_2$ tablespoons
1 oz yeast, granulated = 1 level tablespoon

American Measures

16 fl oz	=1 American pint
8 fl oz	=1 American standard cup
0.50 fl oz	=1 American tablespoon

(slightly smaller than British Standards Institute tablespoon)

0.16 fl oz	=1 American teaspoon

Australian Cup Measures

(Using the 8-liquid-ounce cup measure)

1 cup flour	4 oz
1 cup sugar (crystal or caster)	8 oz
1 cup icing sugar (free from lumps)	5 oz
1 cup shortening (butter, margarine)	8 oz
1 cup brown sugar (lightly packed)	4 oz
1 cup soft breadcrumbs	2 oz
1 cup dry breadcrumbs	3 oz
1 cup rice (uncooked)	6 oz
1 cup rice (cooked)	5 oz
1 cup mixed fruit	4 oz
1 cup grated cheese	4 oz
1 cup nuts (chopped)	4 oz
1 cup coconut	$2^1/_2$ oz

Australian Spoon Measures

	level tablespoon
1 oz flour	2
1 oz sugar	$1^1/_2$
1 oz icing sugar	2
1 oz shortening	1
1 oz honey	1
1 oz gelatine	2
1 oz cocoa	3
1 oz cornflour	$2^1/_2$
1 oz custard powder	$2^1/_2$

Australian Liquid Measures

(Using 8-liquid-ounce cup)

1 cup liquid	8 oz
$2^1/_2$ cups liquid	20 oz (1 pint)
2 tablespoons liquid	1 oz
1 gill liquid	5 oz ($^1/_4$ pint)